TEACH YOURSELF BOOKS

ENGLISH GRAMMAR

The aim of this book is to provide the reader
with a sound understanding of English Grammar so that he may express himself with greater
clarity and accuracy, both in speech and in
writing, and enjoy an added confidence in his
ability to make himself understood. The function and usage of the different parts of speech
are fully explained, and there is a clear expo-
sition of sentence analysis. Extracts from
English literature illustrate the points raised,
and each chapter contains exercises and a
revision paper, the answers to which are given
at the back of the book. The approach is lively
throughout and emphasis is laid on relating the
construction of the English language to modern
idiom.

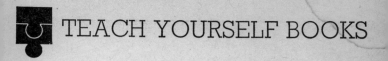

TEACH YOURSELF BOOKS

ENGLISH GRAMMAR

Gordon Humphreys, M.A.

ST. PAUL'S HOUSE   WARWICK LANE   LONDON EC4P 4AH

First printed   1945
This impression   1973

ISBN 0 340 05575 8

*Printed in Great Britain for The English Universities Press Ltd
by T. and A. Constable Ltd, Hopetoun Street, Edinburgh*

PREFACE

" Whatever foreign languages a man meddles with," said John Locke, " that which he should critically study and labour to get a facility, clearness and elegancy to express himself in, should be his own."

This worthy counsel raises some interesting points in support of the study of the grammar of the English Language. In the first place, Locke's plea that English, being our own language, deserves close critical study is most praiseworthy. In the second, his claim that a knowledge of the language can assist in the clarity and elegance of expression cannot be denied ; in the third, it has frequently been admitted that a student learning a foreign language is often better equipped for the task when he has a background of grammar to work upon. Other reasons for the study of the language beyond these may suggest themselves to the reader, not the least of which is that a knowledge of grammar should be followed by greater accuracy of expression. A speaker or writer who knows the rules enjoys an added confidence.

The grammar of a language must not be regarded as a set of principles, however, upon which one construction is absolutely right and another is equally wrong. The language came before the grammar, not the grammar before the language. The grammar of a language explains how a language functions ; as the language progresses, so the grammar develops. The English language is a living language, a workmanlike vehicle of expression which throughout its history has been continually enriched by influences and changes. Disraeli was fond of saying that the English Constitution was a continuative society ; the language of the nation is similarly continuative. With a rich and respected history it is continuously in the process of adapting influences and always reaching after greater simplicity and clarity. So in this book English Grammar is regarded as the grammar of a living language. Throughout, an attempt has been made by a practical approach to relate the constructions of the language to modern idiom.

Every subject dealt with in this series of works has a certain number of technical terms, and English Grammar is no exception. The terms used, however, are introduced to make description and reference simpler, not merely for their own sake.

Each chapter of " Teach Yourself English Grammar " is followed by a revision paper which should be completed satisfactorily before the student passes on to the next chapter.

One of the earliest teachers of English Grammar said nearly four hundred years ago that " without doubt grammatica itself is sooner and surer learned by examples of good authors than by the naked rules of grammarians." Frequently, therefore, the student will be introduced to passages of accredited authors which are examples of the constructions under consideration. He will then be asked to use the construction in many forms himself, to make his own phrases, to suggest his own illustrations of a rule or a principle. His studies should be supplemented, as Ascham advised, by reading, as wide and varied as opportunity permits and interest suggests.

The intention has been to make an interesting approach to the study of English Grammar. Grammar need not be dull. It is hoped that the student as he progresses through the book may find his interest sustained. He may even get some fun out of it.

My thanks are due to my friend Mr. J. Westgate Smith for his helpful suggestions, and to Mrs. David Douglas for her painstaking work on the manuscript.

G. S. H.

Woking, Surrey.

TABLE OF CONTENTS

CONTENTS

CHAPTER I

THE SENTENCE

I. Phrases and Sentences

A large part of our life is spent in transferring our own thoughts to others. There are quite a few ways in which we may do this. We can express our dislike of the medicine prescribed for us by a strained facial expression ; we can emit a sound of pain if we receive a blow ; we can draw a map showing a friend the way to a certain place. In the realm of Art, the painter transfers his thoughts to canvas, the sculptor to marble and the composer to music.

But the commonest form of expressing ourselves is, of course, in words. The small child uses just single words and the admiring parent is delighted to hear the signs of growing intelligence in the child as it begins to say, " Dada," " Light," " Hot." In the course of time, the child is able to frame groups of words which make *complete* sense. Such groups of words are called *Sentences*. Not all groups of words are sentences. For instance, consider the following groups of words :

(i) The the over moon cow jumped.
(ii) A in saves nine stitch time.

Such groups do not make sense—they are mere collections of words.

Again, consider the groups

(i) over the moon ;   (ii) to see such fun.

These groups make sense, but the sense is not complete. The words do not express a whole idea. Such groups of words, making sense but not complete sense, are called *Phrases*.

II. Sentences

Consider a Third Group :

(i) The cow jumped over the moon.
(ii) The little dog laughed to see such fun.

These groups of words make complete sense. They are called *Sentences*. A sentence, therefore, may be called a group of words which makes complete sense and expresses a complete thought.

Exercise 1.—State which of the following groups of words are sentences and which are phrases :

1. The old grey goose is dead.   2. She died last Friday.
3. With a pain all in her head.   4. Go and tell Aunt Nancy.
5. To make her feather-bed.   6. Old gander is weeping.

Exercise 2.—Construct sentences from each of the following phrases (e.g. to the Fair. On Saturday afternoon we all went to the Fair) :

1. Along the road.   2. Five yards of ribbon.   3. Driving furiously.   4. The house, together with the garden and garage.   5. The weather being hot.   6. To be a farmer's boy.

III. The Full Stop and Capital

If we find that we need more than one statement about the idea that is in our minds, we begin another sentence, whether it refers to the same person or thing or to a different one. To avoid confusion between sentences, a full stop (.) appears at the end of each sentence, and the next sentence begins with a capital letter.

There were not such divisions in early writings. If the methods of those days were still followed today, the well-known passage from St. Luke would read : *my soul doth magnify the Lord and my spirit hath rejoiced in God my saviour for he hath regarded the lowliness of his handmaid for behold from henceforth all generations shall call me blessed for he that is mighty hath magnified me and holy is his name.*

Punctuation and capital letters make reading of modern texts much easier.

Exercise 3.—The following passages consist of sentences which have not been separated. Rewrite the passages, putting a full stop at the end of each sentence and a capital letter at the beginning of each new sentence :

(i) Mole thought his happiness was complete when, as he meandered aimlessly along, suddenly he stood by the edge of a full-fed river never in his life had he seen a river before—this sleek, sinuous, full-bodied animal, chasing and chuckling, gripping things with a gurgle and leaving them with a laugh, to fling itself on fresh playmates that shook themselves free, and were caught and held again all was ashake and ashiver—glints and gleams and sparkles, rustle and swirl, chatter and bubble the mole was bewitched, entranced, fascinated.—KENNETH GRAHAME, "The Wind in the Willows."

(ii) We had a narrow escape a wave appeared high above the rest, and there was the usual moment of intense exertion it was of no use and in an instant the wave seemed to be hurling itself upon us with a yell of rage the steersman struggled with his oar to bring his prow to meet it he had almost succeeded when there was a crash and a rush of water round us I felt as if I had been struck upon the back with knotted ropes while foam gurgled round my knees and eyes.—J. M. SYNGE, "The Aran Islands."

IV. Kinds of Sentences

Consider the following sentences :

1. Too many cooks spoil the broth.
2. Where are you going to, my pretty maid ?
3. Give me the daggers.
4. What a dark night it is !

In example 1 the sentence takes the form of a *statement* or assertion about *cooks*. In example 2 the sentence takes the form of a *question*. In example 3 the sentence takes the form of a *command*. In example 4 the sentence takes the form of an *exclamation*. A sentence may be, then, one of four kinds : (i) a statement ; (ii) a question ; (iii) a command (desire, request, wish) ; (iv) an exclamation.

Exercise 4.—Pick out sentences in the form of statements, questions, commands, exclamations in the following passage :

Alice waited for some time without hearing anything more. At last came a rumbling of little cart wheels, and the sound of a good many voices all talking together : she made out the words : "Where's the other ladder ?—Why, I hadn't to bring but one ; Bill's got the other.—Bill !

Fetch it here, lad. Here, put 'em up at this corner.—No, tie 'em together first—they don't reach half high enough yet.—Oh! they'll do well enough ; don't be particular.— Here, Bill! catch hold of this rope.—Will the roof bear ? Mind that loose slate.—Oh! it's coming down ! Heads below ! (A loud crash.)—Now, who did that ?—It was Bill."   " Alice in Wonderland."

Exercise 5.—State the kind of each of the following sentences (statement, question, command, exclamation) :

1. I do not like thee, Doctor Fell.   2. Does he live on turnips, tea or tripe ?   3. Does he like his shawl to be marked with a stripe ?   4. Beautiful soup, so rich and green, waiting in a hot tureen, who for such dainties would not stoop ?   5. Play a straight bat.   6. What victories we all gain in Dreamland !   7. Life all depends upon the liver. 8. Stand fast.   9. What part are you taking ?   10. What nonsense you talk !

Exercise 6.—Write four sentences, one a statement, one a question, one a command, one an exclamation, about each of the following :

(E.g. Statement : Coal is one of the chief natural resources.
       Question : What is its price per ton today ?
       Command : Shoot the coal on the dump.
       Exclamation : How brittle this coal seems !)
       Tennis, cycling, swimming, wind, money.

V. Parts of the Sentence : Subject and Predicate

(i) Consider the following sentences :

     1. The Jackdaw sat on the Cardinal's chair.
     2. Bishop and abbot and prior were there.

Each of these sentences can be divided into two parts.

1st Part	*2nd Part*
1. The Jackdaw	sat on the Cardinal's chair.
2. Bishop and abbot and prior	were there.

The 1st Part names what we are thinking about in the sentence : e.g. *The Jackdaw* ; *Bishop and abbot and prior*. This part of the sentence is called the *Subject*.

The 2nd Part of the sentence makes a statement about the subject : e.g. *sat in the Cardinal's chair* ; *were there*. This part is called the *Predicate*.

In every sentence, whether it is a statement, question, command or exclamation, there is the subject, which names the person or thing we are thinking about, and there is the predicate, which states what we are thinking about the subject.

(ii) In a *Question-sentence*, the order of words may be different from the normal order of words in a statement-sentence ; but the two essential parts of the sentence, the subject and predicate, are there : e.g. Has anyone seen Harry ?

Subject	*Predicate*
Anyone	Has seen Harry ?

(iii) In a *Command-sentence*, the subject is only rarely mentioned but it is always quite clear that the subject is *you*. When you see the instruction " Keep off the grass," it means " *You* keep off the grass." In command-sentences we say that the subject is *understood*. It is not in the sentence but is understood as being there.

Subject	*Predicate*
(You)	Keep off the grass.

(iv) In an *Exclamation-sentence*, the normal order again is often reversed : e.g. How brittle this coal seems !

Subject	*Predicate*
This coal	seems how brittle !

VI. Analysing a Sentence into Subject and Predicate

Three points must be borne in mind in the division or *analysis* of the sentence :

1. The word-order is not necessarily a guide to the division of the sentence. The normal order, (1) Subject, (2) Predicate, may be altered for purposes of emphasis. Lord Palmerston is reputed to have written across a public despatch, " Sentences should . . . begin with the nominative, go on with the verb and end with the accusative."

However, we find that to give variety and force to our sentences this normal order is frequently disturbed.

E.g. Never home came she.

The analysis of this sentence is :

Subject	Predicate
She	never came home.

The subject has been placed not first, but last, in the sentence.

2. It is advisable to reconstruct in our minds sentences in the form of questions and commands into the normal order of a statement - sentence before deciding on the subject and the predicate : e.g. :

What are you doing ?	You are doing what ?
Stand at ease.	(You) stand at ease.

3. See that all words in the sentence are attached to the part, the subject or the predicate, to which they naturally belong.

Consider two sentences :

(1) The dog curled up before the fire.

Subject	Predicate
The dog	curled up before the fire.

But suppose the sentence reads :

(2) The dog, exhausted after his long chase, curled up before the fire.

Does " exhausted after his long chase " tell us about *dog* or does it tell about the *curling up* ? It describes *dog* ; therefore it belongs to the subject. Does " before the fire " tell us about the *dog* or the *curling up* ? It says *where* the dog curled, therefore it belongs to the predicate.

Subject	Predicate
The dog, exhausted after his long chase,	curled up before the fire.

Exercise 7.—Divide the following sentences into subject and predicate :

(*a*) *Statement.*

1. The Cardinal drew off each plum-coloured shoe.
2. They can't find the ring.

3. Two nice little boys, rather more than grown,
   Carried lavender bags and eau-de-Cologne.
4. Never was heard such a terrible curse.
5. In and out, through the motley rout,
   That little Jackdaw kept hopping about.

(b) Question.

1. Who killed Cock Robin ?
2. What made you so awfully clever ?
3. Have you ever seen a dream walking ?
4. What can the matter be ?
5. Is your name Shylock ?

(c) Command.

1. Switch off that light.
2. Mind your head.
3. Step off with the left foot.
4. Quick march.
5. Ask me another.

(d) Exclamation.

1. What a din you are making !
2. How old he is looking !
3. What a funny figure he cuts !
4. How daintily she treads, like a cat on hot bricks
5. With what disdain you glower upon me !

(e) Miscellaneous : Sentences from English Song.

1. Where have you been all the day, Billy boy ?
2. Keep right on to the end of the road.
3. Abide with me.
4. Land of Hope and Glory, mother of the free,
   How shall we extol thee ?
5. God save the King.
6. Britannia rule the waves.
7. Daisy, Daisy, give me your answer, do.
8. How lovely are Thy dwellings !
9. It's a long way to Tipperary.
10. What shall we do with the drunken sailor ?
11. Did those feet in ancient time walk upon England's mountain green ?
12. The Minstrel Boy to the war has gone.

Revision

1. State whether the following are phrases or sentences. State, in the case of the sentences, whether they take the form of a statement, a question, a command or an exclamation :

1. A sentimental passion of a vegetable fashion must excite your languid spleen. 2. With desperate deeds of derring-do. 3. She may well pass for forty-three, in the dusk with a light behind her. 4. For all her golden hair, tarnished with rust. 5. Lookin' at his mammy, wid eyes so shiny blue. 6. Truth for ever on the scaffold, Wrong for ever on the throne. 7. Be valiant, but not venturous. 8. What is so rare as a day in June ? 9. How the rogue roared ! 10. Let thy attire be comely, but not costly.

2. Divide the following sentences into subject and predicate :

1. The pier is near. 2. The bells I hear. 3. Get your weapons ready. 4. Every bullet has its billet. 5. In married life three is company and two none.—(OSCAR WILDE.) 6. Anybody can be good in the country. 7. What dangers he is prepared to run ! 8. How fast has brother followed brother from sunshine to the sunless land ! 9. Abide with me.

10.   Up from the meadows rich with corn,
       Clear in the cool September morn,
       The clustered spires of Frederick stand
       Green-walled by the hills of Maryland.
                                    J. G. WHITTIER.

CHAPTER II

THE NOUN

I. The Subject-Word

The subject of a sentence names the person or thing about which we are thinking. Sometimes the subject is composed of one word : e.g. Birds | were singing in the tree-tops.

But more commonly the subject is formed by a collection of words : e.g. The men at the factory | enjoyed the concert.

But in the collection of words forming this subject there is one word which denotes what we are thinking about— the word *men*. This is called the Subject-word. It is called a Noun because it is a name.

A *noun* is a word which is the name of a person, place or anything : e.g. Shakespeare, Bournemouth, bicycle, rabbit.

The noun is said to be in the *Singular* number if it refers to *one* thing (e.g. bicycle, rabbit). It is said to be in the *Plural* number if it refers to more than one thing (e.g. bicycles, rabbits). A noun which is the subject of a sentence is said to be in the *Subjective* or *Nominative Case*.

Exercise 8.—In the following passages the first nouns are written in italics. Pick out the rest of the nouns, stating whether they are singular or plural number :

(a)   My *Mammy* was a wall-eyed *goat*,
        My *Old Man* was an *ass*,
        And I feed myself off leather boots
        And dynamite and grass ;
        For I'm a mule, a long-eared fool,
        And I ain't never been to school.—ANON.

(b).—On his *deathbed* poor *Lubin* lies, his *spouse* is in *despair* ; with frequent sobs and mutual cries they both express their care. " A different cause," says Parson Sly, " the same effect may give ; poor Lubin fears that he shall die, his wife that he may live."—PRIOR.

(c).—July 11th, 1664. Knowing what *money* I have in the *house*, and hearing a *noise*, I began to sweat worse and worse, till I melted almost to *water*. I rang and could not in half an hour make one of the wenches hear me ; and this made me fear the more lest they might be gagg'd,— and then I began to think that there was some design in a stone being flung at the window over our stairs this evening, by which the thieves meant to try what looking there would be after them and know our company. These thoughts and fears I had and do hence apprehend the fears of all rich men that are covetous and have much money by them. At last, Jane rose, and then I understand it was only the dog wants a lodging and so made a noise.—-PEPYS.

(d)   I wish I were a
Elephantiaphus
And could pick off the coconuts with my nose.
But oh ! I am not
(Alas ! I cannot be)
An elephanti-
Elephantiaphus,
But I'm a cockroach
And I'm a water-bug,
I can crawl around and hide behind the sink.

II. Kinds of Nouns

Read the following passage :

Old London Bridge

Slowly advancing along the bridge, I came to the highest point, and there I stood still, close beside one of the stone bowers in which, beside a fruit stall, sat an old woman with a pan of charcoal at her feet, and a *book* in her hand in which she appeared to be reading with *attention*. There I stood, just above the principal arch, looking with amazement at the scene that presented itself—and such a scene ! Towards the left bank of the river, a *forest* of masts, thick and close, as far as the eye could reach ; spacious wharves surmounted with gigantic edifices ; and far away, Caesar's Castle, with its White Tower. To the right, another forest of masts and a maze of buildings, from which, here and there, shot up to the sky buildings taller than *Cleopatra's*

Needle—vomiting huge wreaths of black smoke which forms the canopy—occasionally a gorgeous one—of the more than Babel city. Stretching before me, the troubled breast of the mighty river, and, immediately below the main whirlpool of the Thames the Maelström of the bulwarks of the middle arch—a grisly pool with its superabundance of horror, fascinated me.—GEORGE BORROW.

There are four nouns italicised in the passage :
> *book,   Cleopatra,   forest,   attention.*

(a) *Book* is the name *common* to a certain class of article. When the word *book* is used, it might refer to any book. *Book* is then said to be a *Common* Noun. *A common noun is a name shared in common by everything of the same class or kind*. Other common nouns in the passage are *bridge, point,* etc.

(b) *Cleopatra* names a particular person, as *Egypt* names a particular place, and the *Cleopatra's Needle* is a particular thing. *The name given to a particular person, place or thing is a Proper Noun*. Proper nouns are distinguished by a capital letter. Another proper noun in the passage is *Thames*. Poets have used proper nouns to produce a powerful musical effect :

e.g.   And what resounds
          In fable or romance of Uther's son
          Begirt with British and Armoric knights
          And all who once, baptized or infidel,
          Jousted in Aspramont or Montalban,
          Damasco or Marocco or Trebisond
          Or whom Biserta sent from Afric shore
          When Charlemain with all his peerage fell
          By Fontarabia.
                          MILTON, " Paradise Lost," I.

You ought to find out how your own name originated, although you must not be disappointed if the result proves a little humiliating. Some family names originate from the trade or craft of the owner : e.g. Forester, Forster, Foster ; Cooper, Cowper. It may be that the form of the word now conceals its origin : e.g. Chapman (one whose occupation was chaffering, chopping, selling. The expression " to *chop* and change " will be recalled). Some folk owe their names to the place or home of an ancestor : e.g. Underhill, Inwood, Bullen (Boulogne), Lancaster.

A number of names are developments from Christian names : e.g. Thomas, Roberts, Hewett (Hewitt, Hewlett) from Hugh, Johnson (son of John), FitzGerald (son of Gerald).

Others have developed from nicknames. We all know how a nickname sticks when once given, in factory, home or school. Today, Mr. Armstrong may be a poor physical specimen, but a forebear of his must have excelled in strength. Mr. Jocelyne may today be a very dignified gentleman, but an ancestor of his must have walked or looked, it is feared, like a *gosling*.

Sometimes a word that usually appears as a common noun may be used as a proper noun. The word *book* is, as we have noted, usually a common noun, but consider it in this sentence : " *My faith lies in the Book," the old preacher said.* Here the word Book refers to one particular book, the Bible. Similarly, nouns usually regarded as proper nouns may be used as common nouns. We have noted that *Cleopatra* was a proper noun, but consider it in this sentence : *As the soldiers swung through the streets of Cairo, many a dark-eyed Cleopatra threw flowers in their path.* In this sentence, we are not thinking of a particular woman named Cleopatra but of any Egyptian beauty.

(*c*) Reverting to the passage at the head of this section you will notice that the word *forest* is italicised. It occurs in the phrase a *forest of masts.* The word *forest*, although singular, refers to a collection of things. It is therefore called a Collective Noun. *A collective noun is a name which stands for a number of things regarded as a whole.*

(*d*) The fourth word italicised in the passage was *attention.* This is the name of a certain state of mind. Similarly, you might have *energy*, being a certain physical condition, and *generosity*, the name of a moral quality. Such names are called Abstract Nouns. Abstract nouns do not refer to objects which can be seen or touched. *An abstract noun is the name given to a state, quality or feeling.*

Order, comfort, regularity, cheerfulness, good taste, pleasant conversation—these are the ornaments of daily life, wrote Benjamin Jowett. How many of the nouns in that sentence are abstract ?

Exercise 9.—(*a*) Pick out all nouns, other than those italicised, in the Borrow passage, and state whether they are Common, Proper, Collective or Abstract.

(*b*) Pick out the nouns in the following announcement that appeared in a provincial newspaper :

" We wish to apologise for the statement of yesterday that Mr. A. B. Smith is a defective in the local Police Force. We should, of course, have stated that Mr. Smith is a detective in the local Police Farce."

Exercise 10.—In each of the following groups of words, find the noun that is different in class from all the rest :

1. convoy, fleet, flotilla, crew, men, unit.
2. joy, grief, tears, regret, endurance, despair.
3. peace, home, room, wife, chair, child.
4. Edinburgh, Fife, Scotland, Bruce, loch, Ben Nevis.

Exercise 11.—What collective nouns are used to denote a collection of sheep, cattle, wolves, partridges, bees, lions, geese, young pigs, whales, teachers, singers, musicians, workmen, rooms, books, mountains, shrubs ?

III. Number

The plural of the majority of nouns is formed by adding " -s " to the singular : book-s, boy-s.

If the noun is a compound word, the -s is added to the important part : sons - in - law, maid - servants, sergeant-majors. Nouns ending in a hissing sound add -es : ash-es, fox-es, dress-es. Nouns ending in -o also usually add -es : Negro-es, cargo-es, potato-es. But note certain exceptions : solos, oratorios, cantos. The plurals of nouns ending in -f, or -fe, vary in form. Some change f–v : knife, knives ; half, halves. Others keep the f : chiefs, roofs. Yet others retain both forms : wharfs, wharves; scarfs, scarves. A few plurals end in -en : children, oxen. Some plurals are formed by the change of the vowel in the singular :

man, men ; mouse, mice. There are some nouns which have the same form in the singular and plural : *sheep, swine, deer.* Sometimes a word borrowed into English from a foreign language retains its original form : e.g. *phenomenon, phenomena ; addendum, addenda.* But if a foreign word comes into popular use the English -s plural is used, sometimes side by side with the original form of the plural : bandits, banditti ; automatons, automata.

Some nouns, because of their meaning, have only a plural form : *trousers, scissors, news.* (Query : Why is *news* followed by the verb in the singular and *trousers* and *scissors* by verbs in the plural ?) Other nouns have two plural forms with a slight variation in meaning : *appendices, appendixes ; pennies, pence.* Yet others change their meaning when they appear in the plural : *manner, manners ; compass, compasses ; spectacle, spectacles ; spirit, spirits ; brace, braces.* Many other examples of each of the foregoing forms and uses of the plural will suggest themselves to the reader.

IV. The Apostrophe

Examine the sentences :

1. The workers returned to the factory.
2. The worker's home was simply furnished.
3. The workers' homes were a mile from the pit-head.

In the first sentence the word *workers* is a noun in the plural number to denote two or more workers. In sentence 2 the word *worker's* indicates that the home belonged to, was possessed by, one worker. The form *worker's* is said to be the *Possessive or Genitive* Case of the noun *worker.* The mark (') is called the apostrophe. If we refer to the homes belonging to two or more workers, the apostrophe is placed after the " s " : *workers'* homes. *Workers'* is then the possessive case in the plural.

V. Gender

In some aspects the English language is more difficult than others. An example of this is the formation of plurals. In the matter of gender, it is simpler than most languages. In English, the gender of the noun is determined by its meaning and not by its form. This is not the case in Latin, for instance. The word for the noun *sailor* is *nauta*, and that is a feminine form. In English, *sailor*, referring to a man, is masculine gender.

There are three genders in English : Masculine, which denotes males ; Feminine, denoting females ; and Neuter, objects with no sex.

The feminine of a noun may be formed in one of three ways. Some nouns add a suffix : author*ess*, hero*ine*, spin*ster*, vix*en*. Some add a prefix to form a compound word : *she*-bear, *maid*-servant, *hen*-bird. A great number of nouns have a different form altogether for the feminine : e.g. boy, *girl* ; king, *queen* ; ram, *ewe*.

Some nouns may refer to either male or female : parent, neighbour, child. These are said to be Common Gender.

Nouns referring to things having no sex are regarded as neuter : table, plough. Also animals, when we are not concerned with them personally or referring to them biologically, are often denoted by a neuter gender. Thus we say : *A cat can see its way in the dark* ; but children recite : *I do love my pussy, her coat is so warm*. A personal interest in a thing which is inanimate may cause it to be regarded as feminine. The sailor speaks of his ship, and the motorist of his car, as *she*.

Exercise 12.—(*a*) Give the plurals of the following : monkey, pony, woman, cod, library, sheaf, contralto, march, waltz, folio, motto, roof, memorandum, onlooker, looker-on, ring-seat, Miss Robinson.

(*b*) Write out the following, putting one word in the possessive case (e.g. The back of a dog—A dog's back) :

1. A friend of a man. 2. The best friend of a boy. 3. The den of lions. 4. The honour of thieves. 5. The achievements of men. 6. Clothes of women. 7. The tail of a fox. 8. The biscuits of the cook.

(*c*) Why have the following irregular forms of the possessive case arisen : for *goodness'* sake ; *Hercules'* strength ; *Moses'* commandment ?

(*d*) Give six examples of words used in the plural only.

(*e*) Find six words other than those given already which change their meaning in the plural form.

Exercise 13.—Give the feminine equivalent of :

boar, buck, colt, fox, stag, gander, drake, monk, bachelor, wizard, earl, poet, lord, gentleman, chauffeur, widower, policeman, signor, student, alien.

Exercise 14 (a).—Supply a synonym (a word having the same meaning) and an antonym (a word having the opposite meaning) of the following : e.g. enthusiasm (synonym, *zeal* ; antonym, *apathy*) :

prosperity, fatigue, strength, generosity, gentleness, courage, contentment, monotony, agreement, sympathy.

Exercise 14 (b).

Mrs. Malaprop was a character in a play written by Sheridan in the eighteenth century. She was constantly confusing words which sounded similar. She became such a well-known figure in Literature that mistakes of this kind have often been called malapropisms (French : *mal à propos*).

In the following sentences, note the noun wrongly used and supply the correct one :

1. The principle then rose to give his report. 2. The caste included Val Gielgud. 3. The chord snapped under the strain. 4. The play was full of illusions to contemporary life. 5. During the war the corvettes petrolled the submarine lanes. 6. The story appeared in the magazines three years ago in cereal form. 7. One of the most famous autobiographies in the world is Morley's "Life of Gladstone." 8. Henry VIII pressed his suite on Anne Boleyn. 9. As it was a special festival each chorister wore a clean surplus. 10. She is only a postman's daughter but she knows how to sort the males.

VI. Parsing the Noun

We have been studying the noun, which is one of the eight parts of speech. To parse (Latin : *pars*, or part) a word is to state what part of speech it is. When we are asked to parse a word, we state the part of speech and its function in the sentence. In parsing a noun we would give the following details :

1. Its kind. 2. Its number. 3. Its gender. 4. Its case. 5. Its reason for being in that case.

As you continue your studies in this book you will be able to give all the information required for parsing a noun.

Revision

1. Divide into subject and predicate. (Taken from very old volumes of " Punch ") :

1. The next train has gone ten minutes ago. 2. Feed the brute. 3. What is better than presence of mind in a railway accident ? 4. Let loose the gorgonzola. 5. I can actually write my name in the dust on the table. 6. You must be well-educated.

7.   Adam
       Had 'em. (Said to be the shortest poem.)

2. Point out the nouns in the following, stating whether they are Common, Proper, Collective or Abstract :

(a)   Three wise men of Gotham
       Went to sea in a bowl.
       And if the bowl had been stronger,
       My song would have been longer.

(b)   There was an old fellow of Trinity,
       A doctor well versed in Divinity.
       But he took to free-thinking
       And then to deep drinking,
       And so had to leave the vicinity.

(c)   There was a young man of Devizes
       Whose ears were of different sizes.
       The one that was small
       Was no use at all,
       But the other won several prizes.

(d)   A swarm of bees in May
       Is worth a load of hay.

(e)   A crowd attracts a crowd.

(f)
> Here lies Fred
> Who was alive and is dead :
> Had it been his father
> I had much rather ;
> Had it been his brother,
> Still better than another ;
> Had it been his sister
> No one would have missed her ;
> Had it been the whole generation,
> Still better for the nation.
> But since 'tis only Fred
> Who was alive and is dead,
> There's no more to be said.
>
> HORACE WALPOLE.

3. Enumerate the ways you have learnt in English of forming

(i) the plural ; (ii) the feminine.

CHAPTER III

THE VERB

I. The Predicate-Word

Consider the sentences:

1. The priest of the parish *lost* his hat.
2. The King *was* in the counting house.

It has already been noticed that in the subject there is usually one word which is the subject-word. In sentence 1 the subject is *the priest of the parish*, the subject-word is *priest*. The predicate which makes a statement about *priest* named in the subject is *lost his hat*. But, of those three words forming the predicate, there is one which tells us what the priest actually did ; it is the word *lost*. This is the predicate-word. In sentence 2 the subject is *the King*, the predicate is *was in the counting house*. The word *was* enables us to say something about the King—that he *was* in the counting house. The word *was* is the predicate-word.

The predicate-word, from the structural or grammatical point of view, is the most important word in the sentence, for it is the word which makes the statement. It is *the word* in the sentence. It is therefore called the Verb (Latin : *verbum*, the word). In the first sentence, the verb expresses action—*lost* ; in the second, it expresses being—*was*. The verb *lost* is sometimes called a *doing* word and the verb *was* a *being* word.

Frequently the verb is expressed, as in the two sentences which have been considered, by a single word, *lost, was*. But very often, to express, for instance, the time of the action, the verb is made up of two, three or even more words:

The priest *lost* his hat.
The priest *has lost* his hat.
The priest *might have lost* his hat.

There is still only *one* verb in each of these three sentences, although it may be made up of two or three words. Occasionally, for the sake of emphasis, or balance, in a sentence, another word is interposed between the words that make up the verb : e.g. I have nearly exhausted my supply of matches.   The verb is *have exhausted*.

Exercise 15.—Name the verbs in the following passage :

" For the airman the mountains glide and glow : they are alive ; they open and close their ranks ; they greet and beckon ; they lift their relative stations and present the winking cups of their crystalline lakes.   When the pilot rises through the morning grey of a valley and sees the sun's bath of flame suddenly above a mountain range, he has a sense that he is beholding the dawn of creation.   A flood of young light pours over the wings of his machine ; peak on peak is touched with fire.   Reddish mist steams up from distant valleys and disperses in the morning breeze."

From PETER SUPF, " The Airman's World."
Translated by Cyrus Brooks.

II. Function

In many instances a word may sometimes be used as a noun and sometimes as a verb.   It may also be used for other parts of speech.   A man may be an *engineer* at his work, a *decorator* in his own home in the evening, an *outside-right* on Saturday afternoon and a *sidesman* on Sunday morning.   He may have many functions.   Similarly a word may be used with different functions : e.g. (1) The Arsenal *beat* the opponents after an exciting game (verb) ;   (2) P.C. 99 continued his *beat* without further excitement.

Exercise 16.—Construct sentences using the following words (i) as nouns ; (ii) as verbs :

part, guard, blow, work, dream, sweep, round, book, help, close.

Exercise 17.—What difference of stress is used in the following words to indicate the difference in function as nouns and verbs :

conduct, convert, convict, contest, combine, escort, transfer, present ?

The English language is rich in verbs—there is a variety to suggest sound, colour and motion. For instance, all creatures move, but the difference in the manner of their movement is indicated by the use of appropriate verbs. Men *walk*, frogs *jump*, peacocks *strut*, ducks *waddle*, lambs *frisk*. Most creatures *eat*, but we say that lions *devour*, turkeys *gobble*, cows *chew*. We occasionally are driven to use one of these verbs, usually associated with these lower creatures, to denote the manner in which some human beings eat their food.

Exercise 18.—Name the creature which would be associated with the sound expressed in the following verb (e.g. neighs—The horse neighs) :

> brays, roars, trumpets, bleats, low, barks, crows, croaks, laughs, hisses, caws.

III. The Object

Consider the sentences :

> 1. The carpenter saws the wood.
> 2. The *Ark Royal* sank off Gibraltar.

There are three ideas in the first sentence : (1) The carpenter, the *doer* of the action ; (2) *saws*, the verb which states the action ; (3) the *wood*, which receives or suffers the action.

Carpenter is the subject of the verb *saws* ; *wood* is said to be the *object* of the verb *saws*. *Saws* is the verb which *carries over* the action from the subject to the object. When a verb takes an object, the verb is said to be *transitively* used (from the Latin word *to go across*, e.g. trans-Atlantic). A noun forming an object is said to be in the Objective or Accusative Case.

Query : What is the case of a noun forming the subject of a sentence ?

In the second sentence, the action of the verb is complete in itself. There is no carrying over. When a verb denotes an action which is complete in itself, the verb is said to be *intransitively* used. The same may often be used either transitively or intransitively : e.g. I *shall return* your manuscript next week (transitively used, object *manuscript*) ; I shall return next week (intransitively used).

IV. Cognate Object

When a verb is followed by an object formed from the same root as the verb (e.g. I *knocked* a loud *knock*), it is known as a *Cognate Object*.

The old rhyme supplies a number of cognate objects :

> So forth to steal he softly stole,
> The bags of chink he chunk,
> And many a wicked smile he smole
> And many a wink he wunk.

V. Verbs with Two Objects

Some verbs may be followed by two objects : (i) I asked *him* the *reason*. (ii) Tell *me* the *truth*. *Reason* and *truth* are sometimes referred to as *direct objects* and are in the Accusative Case. *Him* and *me* are sometimes referred to as *indirect objects* and are said to be in the Dative Case. It will be noted that when the direct object and indirect appear in a sentence, the indirect object appears first.

VI. Verbs of Incomplete Predication

A verb may require an additional word or words (other than an object) to complete the predicate. Some intransitive words (the verb " to be " is a common example) cannot form a predicate by themselves. For example, *The day was* does not make sense. The verb *was* needs another word in the predicate, or a *predicative word* to complete the predicate : e.g. The day was *dull*. Mr. Churchill became *Premier*. Predicative words are sometimes called the complement.

> *Query :* What case is the noun *Premier*, nominative or accusative ?

Exercise 19.—State whether the verbs used in the passage in Exercise 15 (as far as *dawn of creation*) are transitively or intransitively used.

Exercise 20.—Construct sentences using the following words, first transitively and then intransitively: e.g. We *turned* the corner (transitively used); The tide *has turned* (intransitively used):

hear, talk, move, wave, win, write, recover, rest, melt, drive.

Exercise 21.—Point out the predicative words in the following:

1. You are old, Father William. 2. I am twenty-one today. 3. They seemed friendly. 4. The rogues have turned traitors. 5. With a few weeks' practice, we shall become experts. 6. Smith was our first choice.

VII. Person and Number

(*a*) *Person*—Verbs are said to have three persons, as follows:

First person—the person or persons speaking of himself, herself or themselves: e.g. *I like strawberries. We like strawberries.*

Second person—a person being spoken to: e.g. *You like strawberries.* In olden days the form was sometimes used in the singular: *Thou likest strawberries.* This form is now reserved for devotional use.

Third person—the person(s) or thing(s) spoken of: e.g. *He (she, it) likes strawberries; They like strawberries.*

The old third person singular ending in -*eth* (*My Father knoweth*) has now disappeared except, again, in devotional use.

It is most important to see that the number and person of the verb agree with the number and person of the subject. "Some folks *gets* the fat and some *gets* the lean as they goes on their journey through life" may be a wise observation on life, but it is ungrammatical. In some parts of England it is not uncommon to hear, "The grocer have mislaid my order," and "We butchers knows our trade."

Exercise 22 (a).—Supply from the words in brackets the correct form of the verb in the following :

1. The guard — his whistle (blow, blows).   2. The passengers — into their seats (settle, settles).   3. The driver and the fireman — the track well (know, knows). 4. The train with its load of passengers — slowly through the London suburbs (move, moves).   5. There — a flock of birds, frightened by the shrill whistle (go, goes).   6. A herd of cattle — undisturbed (was, were).

(b) *Number : Double or Multiple Subject.*—Sometimes two or three or more nouns are linked together to form a double or multiple subject.

Jack and Jill went up the hill.   (Double subject.)
Mary and Tom, Joan and Rex were elected to represent the
   side in the Doubles Championship.   (Multiple subject.)
   Query : The following are idiomatic forms in English.
   Why is the singular used ?
   1. Fish and chips *is* a popular Cockney supper.
   2. All work and no play
      Makes Jack a dull boy.
   3. Milk and cinnamon *is* good for a cold.

(c) *Number : Collective Nouns.*—When the subject is a collective noun in the singular the verb that follows is in either the singular or plural according to the meaning required in the sentence :

e.g. (i) The crew was well trained.
     (ii) The crew were made up of English, French,
          Indians and Lascars.

In sentence (i) the crew is regarded as an entity, one unit. So the verb appears in the singular. In sentence (ii) the crew are regarded as a number of individuals. So the plural is used.

   Query : Have you any criticism of the following ?
   1. The nation *was* facing *their* worst ordeal.
   2. The council *are* giving the matter *its* immediate
      attention.
   3. The Board of Directors *is* convinced that *they*
      will have the support of the workers in this
      new scheme.

(*d*) *Nouns with a Plural Form.*

  (i) *Mathematics is* a compulsory subject for this examination.
  (ii) The *gallows is* ready.

Each of these nouns has a plural form, but mathematics is the name of one subject, and gallows is the name of one instrument. So they are regarded as singular.

  Query : Suggest other words that have a plural form but a singular sense.

(*e*) *Either . . . or, neither . . . nor.*—These words which suggest an alternative are followed by the singular, provided they refer to alternative nouns in the singular, as are : *every, everyone, everybody, nobody,* etc.

  e.g. Everyone was ready for action.   Nobody was absent.
       Everything is in its proper place.   Neither his brother nor his sister was prepared to help him.

Exercise 22 (b).—Supply the correct form of the verb in the following :

  1. Tripe and onions — an enjoyable dish (is, are).
  2. "Tom, Dick and Harry" — one of Talbot Baines Reed's popular books (is, are).
  3. A whisky and soda — his favourite night-cap (was, were).
  4. Physics — the subject in which he was specialising (was, were).
  5. The scissors — blunt (is, are).
  6. The news at last — ground for real hope (give, gives).
  7. Either Smith or Brown — at the piano (is, are).
  8. Everyone — making for the door (was, were).
  9. The team — drawn from England, Scotland, Wales and Ireland (was, were).
  10. The school — assembled by nine o'clock (was, were).

VIII. Tense of the Verb

Consider the following sentences :

  1. Mr. Brown walks with a limp.
  2. Mr. Brown walked with a limp.
  3. Mr. Brown will walk with a limp.

In sentence 1 the verb expresses an action going on in present time. It is said to be in the Present *Tense*. (Latin : *tempus*, time.) The verb in sentence 2 expresses an action going on in past time. It is said to be in the Past Tense. The action of the verb in sentence 3 expresses an action going on in future time. It is said to be in the Future Tense. The point must now be studied a little more closely.

(*a*) *Present Tenses*.—(i) Mr. Brown *walks* with a limp. (ii) Mr. Brown is walking with a limp. (iii) Mr. Brown has walked with a limp.

In sentence (i) the Simple Present Tense is denoted. In sentence (ii) the action is in present time, but there is an emphasis on the fact that the action is continuing. In sentence (iii) the action is completed or made perfect in present time. The three tenses are called therefore : (i) *walks*—Present Simple ; (ii) *is walking*—Present Continuous ; (iii) *has walked*—Present Perfect. Read the following passage, first in Present Simple, then in Present Continuous, and lastly in Present Perfect Tense :

Present Simple	*Present Continuous*	*Present Perfect*
The oldest inhabitant lives in the house by the bridge. He knows everything that goes on in the village. If the Vicar's cat dies, Old Gummidge gives the exact details of its demise to any who wish to know. Gummidge walks along the village streets proudly with the air of a man who claims to be the first to pass on any tasty morsel of information. He listens, puts a few questions and then retells with a few embellishments of his own. No one accepts his stories as they stand. They find great interest in them, however, for the old man tells a good yarn.	The oldest inhabitant is living in a house by the bridge. He is knowing everything that is going on in the village. If the Vicar's cat is dying, Old Gummidge is giving exact details of its demise to any who are wishing to know. Gummidge is walking along the village streets proudly with the air of a man who is claiming to be the first to pass on any tasty morsel of information. He is listening, is putting a few questions and then is retelling with a few embellishments of his own. No one is accepting his stories as they are standing. They are finding great interest in them, however, for the old man is telling a good yarn.	The oldest inhabitant ha lived in a house by the bridge. He has known everything that has gone on in the village. If the Vicar's cat has died, Old Gummidge has given exact details of its demise to any who have wished to know. Gummidge has walked along the village streets proudly with the air of a man who has claimed to be the first to pass on any tasty morsel of information. He has listened, has put a few questions and then has retold with a few embellishments of his own. No one has accepted his stories as they have stood. They have found great interest in them, however, for the old man has told a good yarn.

It may sound paradoxical, but the form of the present tense is sometimes used to make more vivid action in past time : e.g. East and West and South and North, the messengers *ride* fast. This is called the Historic Present.

Similarly, we sometimes use the present tense to express the future : e.g. The sun *rises* at eight minutes past six tomorrow. So, by usage, the same tense form may refer to more than one time.

Exercise 23.—State exactly what the various italicised forms of the present tense denote in the following sentences :

1. The sun *shines* bright.   2. It *is* an Ancient Mariner, He *stoppeth* one of three.   3. Too many cooks *spoil* the broth.   4. The earth *is* round.   5. Shakespeare *says* that who steals my purse steals trash.   6. We *start* work to-morrow.   7. She *is working* in the hay-field.   8. The country *is looking* to its youth for a lead.   9. I *have finished* my course.   10. *Has* Jones *arrived* yet ?

(*b*) *Past Tenses.*—Consider the following : (i) The tourist visited Cheddar Gorge. (ii) The tourist was visiting Cheddar Gorge. (iii) The tourist had visited Cheddar Gorge.

The tense of the verb in sentence (i) is the *Past Simple Tense*. In sentence (ii) the action is in past time, but there is an emphasis on the fact that the action was continuing. The tense of the verb is *Past Continuous*. In sentence (iii) the action is completed or *made perfect* in past time. The tense is known as the *Past Perfect*. The action of the verb often suggests the completion of the action as another begins : e.g. The train *had travelled* nearly a hundred miles before the fire was detected. When the guests *had finished* their meal, the concert began.

Exercise 24.—Write the following passage in indirect speech, commencing : *Daniel Defoe declared that during the plague of London in* 1665, *walking near his brother's warehouse he had questioned a woman whom he had seen* . . .
State the tense of each verb.

" During the plague of London in 1665, walking near his brother's warehouse, he questioned a woman whom he saw coming out with some high-crowned hats. She said there were other people inside, and when Defoe went forward to see she escaped. In the yard he stopped two others carrying stolen hats, so he shut the gate behind him, took the hats from them and asked their business. One acknowledged her error, saying they were told that no one owned the goods. In the warehouse he found several others calmly equipping themselves with hats."

(c) *Future Tenses.*—The future tenses are formed by the use of auxiliary verbs *shall* and *will*.

Consider the sentences : (i) I shall answer your letter in the evening. (ii) I shall be answering your letter in the evening. (iii) I shall have answered your letter in the evening.

The verb in sentence (i) is in the *Future Simple*. The verb in sentence (ii) denotes an action that is going on in future time. It is the *Future Continuous Tense*. The verb in sentence (iii) denotes an action that will have been completed at some point of time in the future. It is the *Future Perfect Tense*.

Shall and will.—The auxiliary verbs *shall* and *will* are used to express futurity as follows :

1st Person.	I shall	We shall
2nd Person.	You will	You will
3rd Person.	He will	They will

Sometimes *shall* is used in the second and third person to express obligation : e.g. Thou *shalt* not steal. *Will* may be used in the first person to express willingness or determination : e.g. I *will* go, whatever you say.

Exercise 25.—Say what the function of *shall* and *will* is in the following sentences :

1. I shall be twenty-one tomorrow. 2. You shall never darken these doors again. 3. You shall have a rise next week. 4. Johnny shall have a new master. 5. You will be on the sea by this time tomorrow. 6. I will not listen to any more complaints. 7. I will all the property to my nephew. 8. I'll go for you.

(d) *The Future in the Past.*—This sounds a strange contradiction of terms. How can the future be in the past ?

Consider the following : (i) " I shall travel on the night train," declared the reporter. (ii) The reporter declared that he *would travel* on the night train. The verb *shall travel* is the Future Simple Tense. The verb *would travel* is said to be the Future in the Past, because it indicates an action

which at some time past was then rightly regarded as
future. All the four future tenses may be regarded in the
past as :

Future Simple in the Past :	He would travel.
Future Continuous in the Past :	He would be travelling.
Future Perfect Continuous :	He would have been travelling.

To put the matter of the tenses of the verb in another
way :

Simple Tenses :

Present Simple :	I write.
Past Simple :	I wrote.
Future Simple :	I shall write.
Future Simple in the Past :	I should write.

Continuous Tenses :

Present Continuous :	I am writing.
Past Continuous :	I was writing.
Future Continuous :	I shall be writing.
Future Continuous in the Past :	I should be writing.

Perfect Tenses :

Present Perfect :	I have written.
Past Perfect :	I had written.
Future Perfect :	I shall have written.
Future Perfect in the Past :	I should have written.

Exercise 26.—State the tense of the verbs in the following
passage :

Smith had been boasting all the evening at the club of
his exploits when he had hunted wild beasts in Africa.
" I am telling you what I have actually seen for myself,"
he declared. "After a few weeks' rest I shall return to the
jungle, as I long for more adventures." Brown then asked
him if he had ever visited Egypt.

"Egypt !" replied Smith. "I visited Egypt six years
ago. I shall be staying at Cairo for a few weeks on my
way to the Jungle. How well I remember that visit to
Egypt ! "

"What happened ? " asked Brown.

" I'll tell you," answered Smith, who beamed at the prospect of another story. " I had gone to Egypt to meet Bloggs, who had promised that he would allow me to assist in some excavations he was making there. Well, I made some wonderful discoveries."

" Really ! " drawled Brown.

" Yes. One was specially notable ; I found skeletons of Pharaoh's lean kine in Egypt."

At this Brown burst out laughing.

" What are you laughing at ? " demanded Smith. " I am telling you the truth."

But Brown could not speak for laughing.

Query : What *was* Brown laughing at ?

(e) *Lie, Lay.*—Some people find difficulty in distinguishing between the verbs *to lie* and *to lay*.

To lie is intransitive ; its simple past tense is *lay* ; its past participle *lain* :

e.g. I lie down on the grass.   (Present Simple.)
     I am lying on the grass.   (Present Continuous.)
     I lay on the grass.   (Simple Past.)
     I had lain on the grass.   (Past Perfect.)

To lay is transitive ; its simple past is *laid* ; its past participle is *laid* :

e.g. I lay my head on the pillow.   (Present Simple.)
     I am laying my burden down.   (Present Continuous.)
     The hen laid five eggs last week.   (Past Simple.)
     The waitress had laid the table.   (Past Perfect.)

IX. Voice

(a) Consider the following sentences :

  (i) The hunter shot the tiger.
  (ii) The tiger was shot by the hunter.

Although there is the same meaning in each sentence, there is a slight difference of emphasis. In sentence (i) the attention is specially on the *hunter*, which is the subject of the sentence. In sentence (ii) it is on the *tiger*, which is the subject in sentence (ii).

Sentence (i) may be divided thus :

Subject	Predicate
The hunter	shot

the tiger (object)

In sentence (ii) it will be noticed that the original object has become the subject, *tiger*.

When a verb represents its subject as doing the action, it is said to be in the Active Voice : e.g. The hunter *shot* the tiger.

When a verb represents its subject as being acted upon, it is said to be in the Passive Voice : e.g. The tiger *was shot* by the man.

So the voice of the verb shows the kind of relationship that exists between the subject and the verb.

Sometimes the passive voice is used because the subject of the verb in the active voice would be unknown : e.g. He *was condemned* to the salt mines.

> *Query :* (If you speak French) How is the passive voice formed in French ?

(*b*) *Retained Object.*—It will be remembered that some verbs can take two objects : e.g. The employer *gave* Jones the sack.

If the sentence is put in the following passive form, it reads : " Jones was given the sack by his employer."

It will be seen that the indirect object (*Jones*) has become the subject. The other object (*sack*) has been retained. *Sack* is called the *Retained Object*.

It is interesting to notice that some nouns have an active and a passive sense : e.g. employer (one who employs) and employee (one who is employed). Other examples are : examiner, examinee ; creator, creation ; eater, eatable ; scribe, script.

The student will be able to supply a list of other examples.

Exercise 27.—Point out the verbs in the passive voice in the following sentences. State the sufferer of the action :

1. The townsfolk were angered at the proposal. 2. The Mayor is supported by the aldermen. 3. They will be

opposed by some members of the Council. 4. Have you been informed of the proceedings ? 5. The town is being canvassed for its opinion.

Exercise 28.—Rewrite the following sentences in the passive voice :

1. The landlady supplied us a first-rate meal. 2. Tom reached the summit first at noon. 3. We all took a rest under the shade of a boulder. 4. The guide pointed out the route home. 5. In the gathering darkness the rest of the company lost sight of Tom.

Exercise 29.—State the voice of the verbs in the following sentences :

1. I shall report the matter to the police. 2. My brother was knocked down by a lorry. 3. You have been warned. 4. The man was trapped in the blazing building. 5. Have you ever been to the State Gallery ? 6. They will be sailing for Gibraltar on Thursday. 7. We had finished by noon. 8. His speech was received most favourably. 9. The scarf was knitted in three colours. 10. Millions of gallons of petrol are shipped to these shores annually.

Exercise 30.—Rewrite the following in the passive voice, underlining any retained objects :

1. The old shepherd showed us a short cut. 2. Robin paid the old rogue five pounds for that cycle. 3. The Police offered the finder a reward of ten shillings. 4. His enemies asked him no further questions after that rebuff. 5. That will teach him a lesson.

Exercise 31.—Correct the form of the passive voice where necessary in the following sentences :

1. The Mayor was beseeched to intervene. 2. The spy will be hung at dawn tomorrow. 3. The audience was bade to remove hats. 4. An interesting play was broadcasted last night. 5. Such a burden could not be born indefinitely. 6. The ship was broke up. 7. The horse has been rode too hard. 8. Half of the meal had been ate.

9. The egg has been lain for over a month.   10. The stain had been trod all over the carpet.

X. Kind.—Strong or Weak

The old Grammarians divided verbs into two conjugations, strong and weak. It is interesting to understand what they meant by these terms. Consider the verbs *sing* and *dance*.

> Sing :   Past Simple Tense, *sang*. (Strong verb.)
> Dance : Past Simple Tense, *danced*. (Weak verb.)

Verbs forming the past tense by a vowel change are called Strong Verbs. They are principally the old monosyllabic words of our own language. Verbs forming the past tense by the addition of the suffix -ed, -d or -t are called Weak Verbs. Actually this ending is an abbreviation of the past tense of " do," *did* :

> I danced—I dance did.

It might be noted that some weak verbs shorten the vowel as well as employ the suffix to form the past tense : e.g. tell, told.

Also some verbs whose present tense already ends in -d or -t retain the same form for the past tense : e.g. cut, cut ; rid, rid.

Exercise 32.—Classify the following verbs as strong or weak :

(1) begin, (2) commence, (3) speak, (4) talk, (5) win, (6) gain, (7) rise, (8) rear, (9) cut, (10) sever.

XI. Mood

A. FINITE AND NON-FINITE.

Consider the verb in the following sentence : " The monkey *swung* gaily on the bough." Is *swung* present, past or future tense ? Is it singular or plural ? Is it first, second or third person ? *Swung* has a number, person and tense. It is *limited* to its number, person and tense. It is used as a predicate-word with the subject of the sentence. A verb thus limited is said to be *finite*.

B *

Man is sometimes spoken of as finite because he is limited in his function. But we refer to space as infinite because it is limitless. Now consider :

(i) Seeing the monkey, I joined the crowd of spectators.

(ii) Seeing the monkey, you joined the crowd of spectators.

(iii) Seeing the monkey, we joined the crowd of spectators.

(iv) Seeing the monkey, they joined the crowd of spectators.

In (i) seeing refers to " I."   (1st Person Singular.)
    (ii) seeing refers to " you."   (2nd Person Singular.)
    (iii) seeing refers to " we."   (1st Person Plural.)
    (iv) seeing refers to " they."   (3rd Person Plural.)

In other words, the form *seeing* can be used in all four instances. The number and person change, but *seeing* is the same. *Seeing* is not used as a predicate-word in the sentence. It is a present or continuous participle.

As *seeing* is not limited to person and number, it is said to be a non-finite part of the verb.

Note similarly the use of the *Past Participle*.

Wearied with their long march, the soldiers soon fell asleep.

The sentence could also read, " the soldiers *fell* asleep," or " the soldiers *will fall* asleep." *Wearied* is not limited by the tense of the verb in the predicate. It is a non-finite part of the verb, the past or perfect participle, formed from the verb " to weary."

Exercise 33.—State whether the verbs italicised in the following sentences are finite or non-finite :

1. *Picking* his way over the strong path, the traveller *made* for the light. 2. *Seizing* my opportunity, I *knocked* the pistol out of his hand. 3. *Suspected* by his colleagues and *hated* by his foes, the statesman *retired* from office without regret. 4. *Holding* on to his lead, the runner *settled* down to his last lap. 5. *Snubbed, mocked, ridiculed*

and *humiliated*, the wretched man *had* little in life to comfort him.

B. FINITE PARTS.

Mood.—A verb may be used in one of three *moods*. Its mood is the form which shows the manner in which the action is represented :

(*a*) When a verb expresses a fact or asks a question, it is said to be in the *Indicative Mood* :

e.g. (i) Nobody *loves* me.
  (ii) The river Weser, deep and wide, *washes* its walls on the southern side.
  (iii) What *shall* we *do* with the drunken sailor ?

(*b*) When the verb expresses a command, it is said to be in the *Imperative Mood*. This may also include a wish or desire :

e.g. *Pass* down the car.
  Pass the pepper, please.
  Save me.

(*c*) *The Subjunctive Mood.*—This mood as a separate form is disappearing in English. It remains in the following types of sentences :

 (i) To express certain forms of a wish :
   Long *may* he *reign* !
 (ii) To express an unfulfilled wish :
   Would I *had died* for thee !
 (iii) In the subordinate clause of a conditional sentence :
   If wishes *were* horses, beggars would ride.
 (iv) In the subordinate noun clause, following a verb expressing a wish :
   The General Purposes Sub-Committee recommend that the question of a new canteen *be* raised at once by the General Committee.

You will hear more of the types of sentences given under (iii) and (iv) later in the book.

In the following table the subjunctive mood of the verb *to be* is given. The forms printed in italics are no longer in common use :

	PRESENT		PAST	
	Indicative	*Subjunctive*	*Indicative*	*Subjunctive*
I	am	*be*	was	were
thou	art	*be*	wast	*wert*
he	is	*be*	was	were
we	are	*be*	were	were
you	are	*be*	were	were
they	are	*be*	were	were

Correct construction.—It will be seen by the foregoing that it is not necessary for every conditional clause introduced by *if* to use the subjunctive mood. The subjunctive should be used only when there is a genuine supposition. Thus :

> If it *rains*, the meeting will be held in the Oddfellows Hall.

The indicative is used here, as the conditional clause contains an open condition which might possibly be fulfilled. But we should say :

> If London *were moved* further up the Thames, it might be freer from attack.

In this sentence, the conditional clause contains a condition very unlikely to be fulfilled. There, the subjunctive is used.

Exercise 34.—Comment on the syntax of the words in italics :

1. If the Lord *be* God, follow Him. 2. *Stand* and unfold yourself. 3. Though He *lead* me through the deepest waters, He will be with me. 4. He is bound to win, *bar* accidents. 5. *Help!* 6. Who *killed* Cock Robin ?

C. NON-FINITE PARTS.

1. *Participles.*—We have already considered the two participles, present or continuous participle (e.g. seeing) and the past or perfect participle (e.g. wearied), as being non-finite parts of the verb.

(a) In the sentence, " Seeing the monkey, they joined the crowd of spectators," *seeing* qualifies *they* and is doing the work of an adjective (cf. p. 115). In the sentence, "*Wearied* with their long march, the soldiers soon fell asleep," *wearied* qualifies *soldier* and is doing the work of an adjective. The participle may be separated from the noun or noun equivalent it qualifies, as in the two foregoing sentences, or it may be next to it : e.g. (i) *blinding* rain, *howling* wind, *advancing* army (continuous participles) ; (ii) *broken* earthenware, *torn* garment, *cut* finger (perfect participles).

Exercise 35.—Supply suitable present or continuous participles to the following (e.g. — rock, jutting) :

— game, — book, — character, — flower, — clothes, — snow, — darkness, — sun, — clouds, — heat.

Exercise 36.—Supply suitable past or perfect participles to the following (e.g. — rock, sunken) :

— toy, — follower, — promise, — victory, — room, — present, — larder, — student, — building, — plan.

Exercise 37.—Point out the participles in the following passages, stating what words they qualify (e.g. Seizing his opportunity, the thief slipped down a back street : *seizing* qualifying *thief*) :

1. I am the singing clown. 2. Down among the dead men. 3. The Cardinal rose with a dignified look. 4. Toiling, rejoicing, sorrowing, onward through life he goes. 5. One crowded hour of glorious life is worth an age without a name. 6. Each in his narrow cell for ever laid, The rude forefathers of the hamlet sleep.

(*b*) As a participle is an adjective it must be *related* either to a noun or a noun equivalent. Examine the sentence : " Being windy, we could not keep our umbrellas open." To what word in the sentence does *being windy* refer ? It certainly does not refer to the subject of the sentence as it ought. The participle is unrelated. The sentence should, therefore, be corrected :

(i) Either by supplying the subject to the participle (e.g. *The weather being windy, we could not keep our umbrellas open*). Such a phrase is known as a Nominative

Absolute Construction, as the construction has a subject (nominative) and the whole phrase is *absolute* or separate from the construction of the rest of the sentence.

(ii) By substituting a clause (e.g. As it was windy, we could not keep our umbrellas open).

Exercise 38.—Correct the following examples of unrelated participles :

1. Arriving late, the best seats had already been secured. 2. Being Wednesday afternoon, the shops were all shut. 3. Standing on the railway platform, a milk churn was pushed on to my foot. 4. Shutting the door with a violent bang, there was a severe protest from the rest of the students. 5. Hoping to reduce his temperature, the new drug was administered forthwith. 6. Regarded as a future Cabinet Minister, his loss of the election came as a disappointment to all his friends.

Exercise 39.—Construct sentences, using the following variant forms of the perfect participle, and illustrate any difference of meaning or use : e.g. Struck by lightning. Stricken with disease.

> gilded, gilt ; knit, knitted ; shaven, shorn ; hanged, hung ; melted, molten ; drunk, drunken ; swelled, swollen.

2. (*a*) *The Infinitive* is another of the non-finite parts of the verb : e.g. (i) He longs to travel. (ii) To travel is a burning passion with him. The infinitive merely names the verb and in these two sentences is used as a noun. In sentence (i) it is the object. In sentence (ii) it is the subject.

(*b*) *The Split Infinitive.*—In Old English and in some modern languages the infinitive is one word : e.g. Old English, *sprecan* ; German, *sprechen* ; French, *parler* ; Modern English, *to speak*. The unity of the infinitive is often broken by the insertion of an adverb : e.g. to *finally* reject ; to *fondly* hope. There are occasions, however, when a split infinitive gives a smoother reading than the grammatically correct form. Thus, to condemn the split infinitive unreservedly is not only pedantic but unjustified.

(c) The Infinitive without " to."—There are some verbs which are followed by an infinitive without " to."

We say : " *I am obliged to refuse* admittance to anyone without a ticket," but " *I must refuse* admittance . . . ," ; *must* is followed by infinitive without *to*. Note also : *I am able to type now.* I *can type* now.

(d) Tenses of the Infinitive.—There are two tenses in the infinitive, the *Present* and the *Perfect*. The Present Infinitive has been already dealt with. The Perfect Infinitive, as the name implies, names the verb in past time : e.g. to have seen ; to have asked. Actually, the perfect infinitive is often used when the present infinitive would be adequate : e.g. *I should have liked to have been there*, when *I should have liked to be there* would have been sufficient.

There is no form for the future infinitive, but the infinitive may represent future action if preceded by *about to* : e.g. *I am about to leave.*

Exercise 40.—Pick out the infinitives in the following sentences :

1. He likes to run with the hare and to chase with the hounds. 2. To mend a puncture is not difficult. 3. I'm standing at the lamp-post at the corner of the street to see a little lady go by. 4. I come to bury Caesar, not to praise him. 5. You cannot enter here. 6. My mother bids me bind my hair. 7. Can you make him understand ? 8. He used to sit down and see his father toil for him. 9. I heard the Prime Minister speak. 10. Let me go, please. 11. It would have been wiser to have taken the lower road. 12. I must have forgotten my manners. 13. She is about to be married. 14. We could have helped him had he asked us.

3. Gerunds.—A Gerund is a Verbal Noun : e.g. *Walking* is a healthy exercise. I prefer *cycling*. The Gerunds are formed from the verbs *to walk, to cycle*.

A gerund of a transitive verb takes an object : e.g. COLLECTING *salvage was a form of national service*. PLAYING *a straight bat is an elementary rule in cricket*.

It will be noted that both the present participle and the

gerund end in *-ing*. There need, however, be no confusion. Consider, for instance :

(i) The *growling* monster turned on its prey.

(ii) *Growling*, the monster turned on its prey.

(iii) The *growling* of the monster terrified the young deer.

In (i) *growling* qualifies *monster* and does the work of an adjective. It is a present participle. In (ii) *growling* is again qualifying the subject *monster*, and is doing the work of an adjective. In (iii) *growling* is the subject of the sentence, subject of verb *terrified*. It is doing the work of a noun ; it is a gerund.

Parsing the Verb.—When a verb is parsed, the following details should be given : 1. Whether strong or weak. 2. Transitively or intransitively used. 3. Voice. 4. Mood. 5. Tense.   6. Number.   7. Person.   8. Its subject. 9. Object (if transitive).

Exercise 41.—Take a passage from a book or newspaper and parse the verbs according to the instructions given above.

Revision

1. What do you understand by a finite verb ?

2. Pick out the finite verbs in the following, naming nouns that are objects of the verbs transitively used :

(*a*)   He that would thrive
              Must rise at five.
              He that hath thriven
              May lie till seven.

(*b*)   I married a wife,
              She's the plague of my life.
              I wish I were single again.

(*c*)   Who killed Cock Robin ?

3. State the mood of the verbs in the following :

(*a*)   Cross Patch,
              Draw the latch,
              Sit by the fire and spin.
              Take a cup
              And drink it up.
              Then call your neighbours in.

(*b*) BISHOP. Who is it that sees and hears all I do and before whom even I am but as a crushed worm ?
PAGE.   The Missus, my Lord.

(*c*) May your shadow never grow less.

(*d*) " We must gie it up, Alfred."
" What, gie up golf ? "
" Nae, mon, nae.   The meenistry."

(*e*) Hi ! James—let loose the gorgonzola.

(*f*)   Most Gracious Queen, we thee implore
          To go away and sin no more.
          But if that effort be too great,
          To go away at any rate.
                    (Epigram on Queen Caroline.)

4. Parse the italicised words in the following :

(*a*) I went out to Charing Cross, to see Major-General Harrison *hanged*, drawn and quartered ; which was done there, he *looking* as cheerful as any man could *do* in that condition.

(*b*) *Hanging's* too good for him.

(*c*)   They carried a net and their hearts were set
          On *fishing* up the moon.

(*d*) How *do* you *do* ?

(*e*) What *shall* we *do* with the drunken sailor ?

5. Name the Voice tense of the verbs in the following :

(*a*) Nearly all our best men are dead ! Carlyle, Tennyson, Browning, George Eliot !—I'm not feeling very well myself.

(*b*) I will be good.   (Queen Victoria.)

(*c*)   Birds in the high Hall-garden
          When twilight was falling.
          Maud, Maud, Maud, Maud,
          They were crying and calling.

(*d*) Thou hast been call'd, O Sleep, the friend of Woe,
          But 'tis the happy who have called thee so.

(*e*) England has saved herself by her exertions and Europe by her example.—PITT.

(f) Sir, I have quarrelled with my wife ; and a man who has quarrelled with his wife is absolved from all duty to his country.

6. What do you understand by the following expressions? Check up your answers by reference to the chapter just studied :

Cognate Object, Retained Object, Verb of Incomplete Predication, Historic Present, Gerund.

CHAPTER IV

THE ADJECTIVE

I. Adding to the Meaning

There has been a watch stolen in the factory of Messrs. Smokingpots Ltd. The detective, Mr. Trackem, is in the Managing Director's Office.

DETECTIVE. I am glad to report that the missing watch has been found in a pawnbroker's shop in Durford.

MANAGING DIRECTOR. Aha! that's good news. Who brought it to the shop?

DETECTIVE. That's the point. The proprietor, Mr. Dothem, said it looked like a factory hand. I suggest that it was one of your men.

MANAGING DIRECTOR. Half a minute, Mr. Trackem, that's not much progress. I have a thousand men working in this factory.

DETECTIVE. Steady! I pursued my enquiries and found that the man who had lodged the watch in the shop was a small man.

MANAGING DIRECTOR. Pooh! Really, Mr. Trackem, you surprise me. I must have two hundred small men in the factory.

DETECTIVE. You are too impatient, Mr. Goldbank. The man was further described as being fat.

MANAGING DIRECTOR. A small, fat man! But, my dear Mr. Trackem, do you realise that at least twenty men would answer to that description? I can think of Podge, Stodge, Dumps. Yes, there must be a score of them. Have you any closer description?

DETECTIVE. Yes. I have discovered . . .

MANAGING DIRECTOR (*impatiently*). Yes, Mr. Trackem?

DETECTIVE. I have discovered that he was ginger-haired.

MANAGING DIRECTOR. A small, fat, ginger-haired man. That must be George Lightfinger who works in the stores department. Mr. Trackem, you are a genius. Oughtn't we to make an immediate arrest?

Little can be learnt from the foregoing episode of the art of criminology, but something can be learnt of a part of speech known as the Adjective. When the famous detective said that one of the factory hands must have stolen the watch, he might have been referring to any one of the thousand. By describing him as *small*, he limited the number to about two hundred. *Small, fat* man limited them to about twenty. But *small, fat, ginger-haired* man reduced the choice to one. The words *small, fat, ginger-haired* described the noun *man*, and by saying more about him limited the application of the word. In this case the application is limited entirely to the unfortunate Mr. Lightfinger. Words which add something to the meaning of a noun and limit its sense in this way are called Adjectives.

Adjectives sharpen a picture as the lanternist focuses his lens. They add beauty, power and reality to the description. Can you recall any lines of poetry which have struck you where the poet has gripped your attention by his appropriate choice of adjectives ? Do you remember Wolfe's " *struggling* moonbeam's *misty* light," or Dickens' " That *sedate* and *clerical* bird, the rook," or Brooke's " The *rough male* kiss of blankets " ?

Refer to any similar expressions illustrating the graphic use of adjectives that you have met in your reading.

II. Epithet and Predicative Adjective

If an adjective is used along with a noun, it is said to be an *Epithet* : e.g. *merry* yarn, *sweet* dream, *grey* mist (from Masefield's " Sea Fever ").

If the adjective is used along with the verb to complete the predicate, it is said to be a Predicative Adjective : e.g. The violets are *sweet*. The sky grew *red*.

Exercise 42.—Supply adjectives appropriate to the following (e.g. bright fire) :

(a) *Epithets*. — judge, — nurse, — doctor, — preacher, — soldier, — fox, — sheep, — mule, — dog, —bee, — shower, — wind.

(b) *Predicative Adjectives*. The shop assistant was —. The price was —. The sea became —. Danger seemed —. The examination was made — for the juniors. The prisoner was proved —.

III. Overworked Adjectives

There is a tendency for some adjectives to be grossly overworked. People who are too lazy or too indifferent to the exactness of language resort automatically to *bad, good, nasty, nice,* when a little thought would suggest a more appropriate adjective which would give richer colour to the picture. Thus we hear that " Aunt Jemima, who is a *bad* patient, is in bed with a *bad* toe. It is particularly *bad* in *bad* weather, and makes her temper *bad,* as it gives her *bad* nights." This would have been more colourful if the adjective *bad* could have been substituted by a more particular word : " Aunt Jemima, who is a *difficult* patient, is in bed with a *poisoned* toe. It is particularly *painful* in *wet* weather and this makes her temper *irritable* as it gives her *disturbed* nights."

Exercise 43.—Substitute a more suitable word for the adjectives in the following :

a nice holiday, a nice boy, a nice smile ; nasty weather, nasty habits, nasty smell ; awful dress, awful noise, awful crowd.

Exercise 44.—Goods made in England are of *English* make, those in Germany of *German* make. Give the adjectives formed from :

Holland, Norway, Spain, Switzerland, Sweden, Cuba, Peru, Paris, Athens, Naples, Vienna, Aberdeen.

Exercise 45.—(i) What adjectives are formed from the following nouns :

(*a*) event, joy, home, talk, moment, mode, mood, demon, serpent, burden, crisis, control, reality, god.

(*b*) Christ, Confucius, Mahomet, Buddha, Caesar, Napoleon, Hitler, Gladstone, Homer, Shakespeare, Milton, Shaw.

(ii) Form two adjectives from each of the following nouns and state any difference of meaning (e.g. child, childish, childlike) :

man, woman, respect, office, luxury, contempt, grace, credit, friend, brute.

(iii) Give the antonym (opposite in meaning) of the following adjectives (e.g. brave, timid) :

learned, dull, cheap, guilty, virtuous, industrious, temporal, safe, hostile, transitory.

(iv) Construct sentences to illustrate the difference in meaning in the following adjectives :

scholarly, scholastic ; venal, venial ; human, humane ; legible, eligible ; earthen, earthly ; judicial, judicious.

IV. Kinds of Adjectives—Quality, Quantity

(a) Adjectives add to the meaning of the noun in different ways. Those we have been considering thus far have answered the question : What kind of ? : e.g. *small* man, *fat* man, *ginger-haired* man. These are called *Adjectives of Quality*.

Others add to the meaning of the noun by answering the question : How many ? How much ? : e.g. *many* men, *two hundred* men, the *thousandth* man. These italicised words are called *Adjectives of Quantity*. *Many* refers to an *Indefinite Quantity*. *Two hundred* and *thousandth* refer to a definite quantity. *Two hundred* is said to be a *Cardinal Numeral*. *Thousandth* states the order ; it is called an *Ordinal Numeral*. Thus adjectives of quantity may be classified as :

      (i) Indefinite
      (ii) Definite   (a) Cardinal Numerals.
                     (b) Ordinal Numerals.

Exercise 46.—Substitute for the adjectives of definite quantity in italics appropriate adjectives of indefinite quantity (e.g. The pilot brought down *thirty-five* enemy planes (definite quantity) ; *many* enemy planes (indefinite quantity) :

1. The destroyer made *six* attempts to ram the boom.
2. The miser had only *two* friends. 3. She was always to be seen on the promenade with her *seven* puppies led behind her. 4. The sun is *ninety-three* million miles away from the earth. 5. *Nineteen* fires were seen burning in the city.

Exercise 47.—Instance well-known expressions which include an ordinal numeral (e.g. first choice, second fiddle, a thousandth chance).

(*b*) There are some interesting usages of some of the adjectives of quantity. For instance, the word *few* can be used in three ways :

   (i) I spent a *few* days in town.
  (ii) I spent *few* days in town.
 (iii) I spent the *few* days of my furlough in town.

A few indicates that I spent some days, if only a few, in town. *Few* emphasises the fact that there were not many. Indeed, in this sense *few* can mean scarcely any. *The few* means all that there were. It should be remembered that *few* is used with reference to numbers, *little* with reference to quantity. Therefore we should say : " We were fewer (not less) in *numbers* than the enemy."

V. Definite and Indefinite Articles

A, an are forms of the numeral *one* but denote what is called the Indefinite Article, as no particular person or thing is referred to. *The* is called the Definite Article because it refers to a particular person or thing. When two or more adjectives qualify the same noun, the article is used before the first adjective only : e.g. *a black and white frock.*

If Mary went to Brighton with a black and white frock in her case, and Betty went with a black and a white frock in her case, Mary took one frock while Betty took two. Similarly, if Colonel Blimp advertises for a jobbing man and gardener, and Colonel Trump advertises for a jobbing man and a gardener, Colonel Blimp wants one man, while Colonel Trump wants two. We are presupposing, of course, that Colonel Blimp and Colonel Trump know their grammar.

Exercise 48.—Point out the adjectives of quantity in the following sentences :

1. He weighs fourteen stone and stands over six feet in his socks. 2. Few and short were the prayers we said. 3. They

had a few vacancies last week ; few people will want to work for such an unscrupulous firm ; the few weeks I worked for them was enough experience for me.   4. A little knowledge is a dangerous thing.   5. Half the estate went to the eldest son ; all the money was divided equally among the other children.   6. Both competitors had some claim to distinction and no little sense of their importance.

Exercise 49.—Improve the following sentences :

1. We had less apples from the tree this year.   2. You are some electrician.   3. The Lion met an Unicorn.   4. I asked for a hotel and was directed to the best in the town.   5. I have written to him umpteen times but he never replies.

VI. Degrees of Comparison

Consider these sentences :

1. Mr. Coppercoin is a rich man.
2. Mr. Silverbit is a richer man.
3. Mr. Goldpiece is the richest man.

Note the uses of *rich, richer, richest*.   In sentence 1 *rich* simply expresses the quality of the adjective.   In sentence 2 *richer* is used to compare Mr. Silverbit with Mr. Coppercoin. He is the richer of the two men.   In sentence 3 note *richest*. When comparing the wealth of the three rich men, Mr. Goldpiece is the *richest*.   These three forms, *rich, richer, richest*, represent three degrees of comparison.   *Rich* is the ordinary form of the adjective.   It is called the *Positive Degree*.   *Richer* is used when one person or thing is being compared with another.   It is called the *Comparative Degree*.   *Richest* is used when one person or thing is above or superior to all others in the particular quality under consideration.   It is called the *Superlative Degree*.

In short words, like *rich*, the comparative degree is formed by adding *-er*, and the superlative degree by adding *-est*, to the positive degree : e.g. *rich, rich-er, rich-est*.   Sometimes the final consonant is repeated : e.g. *thin, thinner, thinnest*.   If the word is a long one, it is usual to form the comparative and superlative with *more* or *most* : e.g. *energetic, more energetic, most energetic*.

Some of the commonest adjectives, however, have irregular comparisons : e.g. *good, better, best ; bad, worse, worst ; little, less/lesser, least ; much/many, more, most ; near, nearer, nearest/next.*

The superlative degree of the adjective is sometimes used not for purposes of direct comparison, but to express a high degree of the quality of the adjective : e.g. He was given a *most cordial* reception ; It was the *sweetest* little cottage. Even in such uses a comparison may be implied (e.g. the sweetest of all cottages imaginable). Some adjectives, owing to their meaning, have no degrees of comparison. For instance, *round.* If article A is rounder than article B, it means that article B is not round, so the adjective is misused. So, strictly speaking, one thing cannot be *more perfect* or *more unique* or *more square* than another.

Exercise 50.—Give the comparative and superlative degrees of the following positive degrees :

> kind, benevolent, loving, good ; pure, holy, innocent, divine ; hard, cruel, evil, bad, wicked ; small, little, tiny ; late, out, far.

VII. Correct Constructions

(i) It must be remembered that when two things are being compared, the comparative is used, not the superlative : e.g. Who is the *older*, John or Mary ? (not *oldest*). Which is the *quicker* of the two ways ? (not *quickest*).

Conversely, the superlative must be used of more than two : e.g. Which is the *shortest* of your three boys ? (not *shorter*).

(ii) Consider the following sentence : *The centre-forward is more skilful than the whole of the team.*

This is an illustration of the loose use of the comparative degree. How can the centre-forward be more skilful than the members of a team of which he is one ? A comparative can only be used to compare one thing with something separate from itself. The sentence could be corrected to : *The centre-forward is more skilful than the rest of the team.*

(iii) Note the following example of an error in the use of the superlative degree : *John is the tallest of his brothers.*

This, again, is obviously incorrect. John cannot be the tallest of a group to which he does not belong. London cannot be the largest of the American cities, as it is not in America ; Milton cannot be the most famous of the French poets, as he is English. John cannot be the tallest of his brothers, as he is not one of *his* brothers. Alter the sentence to *John is the tallest of the brothers*, and the sentence is correct.

Query : In what other way could the sentence be corrected ?

Exercise 51.—Correct the following sentences :

1. The member for Slowtown is a better speaker than all the members of the House of Commons. 2. The Royal Air Force is now the strongest it has ever previously been. 3. He of all others should have been the most sympathetic to me. 4. This was the severest blow we have ever endured before. 5. The United States, which of all other countries has the greatest industrial resources, proved a powerful ally. 6. I think John is best of the two at darts. 7. In these circumstances to attack was more preferable than to retire. 8. As far as the eighteenth and nineteenth centuries are concerned, the latter showed the greatest industrial advancement.

VIII. Other Kinds of Adjectives

The following kinds of adjectives have now been noted :

1. Adjectives of *Quality* answering the question "What kind of . . . ? "

2. Adjectives of *Quantity* answering the question " How many . . . ? "

Further adjectives must now be considered. You will meet these names again in the chapter on Pronouns.

3. Some adjectives add to the meaning of the noun by answering the question " Which ? " Six kinds of adjectives do this :

   (i) Possessive Adjectives : *my* books, *your* cycle, *his* money.

   (ii) Demonstrative Adjectives (the word demonstrative means pointing out as with a finger) : *this* sword, *that* man, *these* flowers.

(iii) Interrogative Adjectives (asking a question) : *which* way are you going ? *what* terms do you offer ?

(iv) Emphasising Adjectives : my *own* work.

(v) Distributive Adjectives : *each* man, *every* ship.

(vi) Exclamatory Adjectives : *what* endurance !

Exercise 52.—Read the following passage, inserting the most suitable adjective of the kind directed.

(Ql=Quality ; Qn=Quantity ; P=Possessive ; D=Demonstrative ; Em=Emphasising ; I=Interrogative ; Di=Distributive ; Ex=Exclamatory.)

Penguins make —P— nests of stones and they offer them as a —Ql— proposal of marriage. You might see an —Ql— hen receive —P— suitor in a —Ql— frame of mind. For some are shrews in looks and nature. You might see the —Ql— male tender an offering, but the —Ql— hen would scold and peck with —Ql— savagery. But —D— behaviour would not discourage the —Ql— suitor. He would continue with —P— —Ql— endearments until the —Ql— hen, after —Qn— refusals, yielded to —P— charms. —Ex— persistence the penguin shows ! At long last, you would see the hen completely —Ql—, with —P— beak in —P— suitor's, sitting on the ground at —P— feet trembling with —Ql— love. —Ql— affairs of —Qn— people are —Ql— to us. —P— —Em— love-making is probably of —Ql— amusement to others.

IX. Parsing the Adjective

When parsing the adjective, state (i) the kind ; (ii) degree, if the adjective can be compared ; (iii) the word it qualifies ; (iv) epithet or predicative use.

Exercise 53.—Read another story about penguins, pick out the adjectives and state their kind :

Penguins are notorious thieves and are not able to look after their own property very long. There is endless robbery always going on in each rookery. One who spent much time watching the habits of these birds said he saw a cock penguin working with great diligence, stealing many stones from neighbouring nests to make his nest. But as soon as he turned to fetch more stones, another rascally thief would appear, would stand by the nest for a few minutes, as if uninterested in the nest-building. Suddenly it would dart, seize the nearest stone and make off. What action did the hen take ? She looked on while her own home was robbed before her very eyes as if she did not understand what was really happening. When the cock bird returned, he made up for his recent loss by a burglarious descent upon another nest.

X. Correct Constructions

Consider the sentence : *Those kind of mistakes ought to be avoided. Kind* is a *singular* collective noun. It should therefore be qualified by *that*, which is singular, not *those*, which is plural. By a loose construction the plural in *mistakes* has been incorrectly anticipated by a plural form in *those*. Note similarly : *these* class of people, *those* type of men, etc.

Exercise 54.—Correct any mistakes you find in the following sentences :

1. The Mayor is the principle man in our town. 2. The giant air liner has duel controls. 3. The car remained stationery for two hours. 4. I have never made friends of those sort of people. 5. It was a miscellaneous collection of stamps. 6. These kind of toys ought not to be given to children.

XI. Adjectival Equivalents

1. Sometimes a word that is usually used as a noun functions as adjective : e.g. the *hen*-bird, *summer* suns, *apple*-tart. These words, although normally used as nouns, are here qualifying words and are, therefore, adjectives.

Exercise 55.—Make use of the following nouns as adjectives (e.g. *Bread* is the staff of Life (noun). *Bread* pudding (adjective)) :

tennis, cricket, book, garden, floor, chalk, grass, door, man, pig.

2. A verb may do the work of an adjective : e.g. *raging* wind, a *grind*-stone, *storm*-troops.

Exercise 56.—Make use of the following verbs as adjectives :

drop, swing, dive, stop, run.

3. A word that usually functions as an adverb may do the work of an adjective :

e.g. He fell *down* (adverb). The *down* train (adjective).

Exercise 57.—Make use of the following adverbs as adjectives :

up, near, above, through, after.

4. A phrase may do the work of an adjective : e.g. (i) The *Royal* Standard. (ii) The standard *of the King*. *Royal* is an adjective qualifying *standard*. In (ii) the phrase *of the King* is used to qualify *standard*. It is called an *Adjectival Phrase*.

Exercise 58.—Replace the adjectives in italics by adjectival phrases (e.g. His clothes were tattered. His clothes were in tatters) :

1. In the dungeon lay a *chained* prisoner. 2. Old Binks has bought the *corner* house. 3. The *distant* hills were covered with a haze. 4. He is a *promising* student. 5. He drives a *high-powered* car.

Exercise 59.—Replace the adjectival phrases in italics by adjectives :

1. They live in a farm at the top *of the hill*. 2. He took the girl *with the flaxen hair* to the Pictures. On the way, both of them, *without hats*, were caught in the rain. He brought home a girl *with ginger hair*. 3. He has a temper *beyond control*. 4. Mind you are *in time*. 5. His reply was *to the point*.

Exercise 60.—For each of the following adjectival phrases, substitute a simple adjective of equivalent meaning :

1. *to be free* from taxation. 2. *given to being deceived*. 3. *able to use either hand*. 4. life *found under the sea*. 5. *inclined to lose one's temper easily*. 6. His manner is *beyond imitation*. 7. damage *beyond repair*. 8. decision *agreed to without exception*. 9. *inclined to believe everything*. 10. a success *at the beginning*.

5. A clause may do the work of an adjective. Consider :
(i) He has an ungovernable temper. (ii) He has a temper
that cannot be governed. *Ungovernable* is an adjective
qualifying *temper*. *That cannot be governed* is the equivalent of *ungovernable* and is therefore an adjectival
equivalent. It will be noted that this group of words has
the essentials of a sentence ; it makes complete sense and
expresses a single thought. But it is a part of a larger
sentence : He has a temper *that cannot be governed*. It is
a sentence *enclosed* within a sentence. It is therefore
called a Clause (Latin : *clausus*, closed). Therefore *that
cannot be governed* is an *Adjectival Clause.*

Exercise 61.—Supply suitable adjectival clauses in the
following sentences (e.g. The explorers were face to face
with a task which . . . could not be overcome) :

1. Joyce was carrying a case which . . .   2. The boy
made a boat which . . .   3. I was offered a book which . . .
4. The man, who . . . , had never been popular at the works.
5. Then I heard such a scream as . . .   6. The boy whom . . .
has made a great success of his job.

Exercise 62.—Pick out the adjectival clauses in the following. Suggest a single adjective which would have conveyed
the same meaning :

1. He made an observation which could be interpreted
   in two ways.
2. She wore a dress which was not suited to the occasion.
3. This was an act of folly for which there was no excuse.
4. There in Bermuda he met the Great Foe from whom
   there is no escape.
5. He is a man who is always in a temper.

Revision

1. What do you understand by—

   (i) Adjectives of Quantity ;
   (ii) Predicative Adjectives ;
   (iii) Superlative Degree ;
   (iv) Epithet ?

2. Read this metrical riddle and answer the following questions :

   (i) Pick out all the nouns and state their class.
  (ii) Pick out all the adjectives and state their class.
 (iii) Pick out two simple sentences in stanza 1.
  (iv) Analyse these two simple sentences into subject and predicate.
   (v) Parse the word *taken* in stanza 3.

Metrical Riddle (= A Kiss)

I am just two and two. I am warm. I am cold,
And the parent of numbers that cannot be told.

. . . . .

I am lawful, unlawful—a duty, a fault—
I am often sold dear, good for nothing when bought.

. . . . .

An extraordinary boon and a matter of course,
And yielded with pleasure—when taken by force.

COWPER.

CHAPTER V

THE PRONOUN

I.

When we were very small and learning how to talk, our vocabulary was limited almost entirely to nouns. " Baby want rattle," or " Daddy love Baby," or " Give Baby Teddy " would be examples of the next stage. As our vocabulary developed, we found that the constant repetition of nouns was both clumsy and unnecessary. Have you heard this before ? " Your brother Bob owes my brother Bob a bob, and if your brother Bob doesn't give my brother Bob that bob that your brother Bob owes my brother Bob, my brother Bob will give your brother Bob a bob in the eye." We have been spared such tangles as these mainly by words used instead of nouns, called PRONOUNS. Instead of repeating the noun we use a word *pro* or *instead* of the noun. A pronoun refers to a person or thing without actually naming it.

The baby who began by saying " Baby want " and " Give Baby " later learns to say " *I* want " and " Give *me*." These words are pronouns.

II. Personal Pronouns

(*a*)   (i) One person speaking of himself says *I* or *me*.

      (ii) Several persons speaking of themselves say *we* or *us*.

(*b*)   A person addressing another person or persons says *you*. (Cf. also p. 31.)

(*c*)   (i) A person speaking to a second person about a third person or thing says *he* or *him*, *she* or *her*, *it*.

      (ii) A person speaking to a second person about several other persons or things says *they* or *them*.

The words italicised are called *Personal Pronouns* : (*a*) are First Person Singular and Plural ; (*b*) Second Person Singular and Plural ; (*c*) Third Person Singular and Plural.

The pronoun can be the subject of the sentence : e.g.

(i) *I* saw three ships ; (ii) *You* are too wise ; (iii) *She* is the darling of my heart :

Subject	*Predicate*
(i) I	saw three ships (*Object*).
(ii) You	are—too wise (*Complement*).
(iii) She	is—the darling of my heart (*Complement*).

The personal pronoun can also be *object*. Note the following :

1. (*a*) The Duchess accompanied the Duke.
   (*b*) She accompanied him.
2. (*a*) The Duke followed the Duchess.
   (*b*) He followed her.

In 1 (*a*) *The Duchess* is the subject of the sentence. In 2 (*a*) *The Duchess* is the object. The form of the word *Duchess* is the same, whether subject or object. In 1 (*b*) the subject is *she*, being a pronoun indicating the Duchess. In 2 (*a*) the object is *Duchess* ; in 2 (*b*) the object is *her*. The form of the object or accusative case in the pronoun is different from the form of the subject or nominative case. Examine the pronoun used to indicate *Jack* in a similar way. The form of the Second Person Singular *thou, thee* has almost disappeared, having been replaced by *you*. It is now heard only in poetry and in devotional language. The Quakers occasionally use this form.

Exercise 63.—The following passage is written in the first person. Rewrite it in the second person beginning "You ..." and then in third person beginning " He . . ." The change of persons will cause alterations of many other words :

" I have lost an old friend. I lost him last Sunday. He came to church with me as he always did and was with me ushered into our usual pew. He is getting a little old now so I took the precaution to set him down next to me with special care. It is true it had been raining hard and I think he was rather wet all through the service.

" Our church was crowded. We had all come to hear a famous preacher. My pew was especially full. I am afraid

C

I took very little notice of my friend during the sermon, but at the end of the service when I looked round for him, he had gone. I reported the matter at once to the verger, who sympathised with me in my loss, but I could do nothing about it. As I went home in the rain, I knew that one of the worshippers was going home dry, under the protection of *my* umbrella."

III. Pronoun Problems

1. *Case.*—We have noted that there is an accusative or objective form of the personal pronoun : e.g. *me*, *us*. Consider this sentence : *Mary accompanied John and me.* What is the verb of this sentence ? What is the subject ? What case is it ? What is the function of *me* ? What case is it ?

It is seen that *me* is (as well as *John*) the object of the verb *accompanied* and is in the accusative case. Thus the form of the sentence too commonly heard, " Mary accompanied John and *I*," is incorrect. *I* is the nominative form ; *me* must be substituted, as it denotes the accusative case for an object.

2. *Ambiguity.* — Consider this sentence : *When they inspected the camp the following morning, they were dead.* This sentence is ambiguous to the point of absurdity. It reads as if the persons referred to in the first *they* are the same as those referred to in the second. A noun must be substituted for the pronoun : *When they inspected the camp the following morning, the prisoners were dead.*

3. *The Predicative Use of Pronouns.*—The pronoun often appears in the complement. What would you say in answer to the question, " Who goes there ? Who is it ? " Would you say " It is *I* " or " It is *me* " ?

From a strictly grammatical point of view, the nominative case " It is I " is correct, as *is* is a part of the verb *to be* and is followed by the case that precedes it. " It is *I* " is commonly used in dignified language, although " It is *me* " is in popular use. There is something of a parallel in the French " c'est moi." Not wishing to be pedantic on the one hand or ungrammatical on the other, you could answer the question, " Who goes there ? " with " It's Binks here."

4. *Order of Pronouns.*—When pronouns of different persons are used together (nouns are regarded as third person) the second and the third persons in the singular precede the first person : e.g. *You* and *I*, *He* and *I*. Courtesy would suggest such an order. The second person precedes the third : e.g. *You* and *he*. In the plural, *we* has first place, *you* the second, and *they* the third.

5. *Alternative Subject.*—If two or more nouns or pronouns are joined in the subject by *or, nor, either . . . or, neither . . . nor*, the finite verb that follows agrees in number and person with the last-named pronoun in the subject :

e.g. (i) Either you or I *am* to blame.
(ii) Neither he nor you *are* ready.

These are the grammatically correct forms, but again English people dislike being thought pedantic and so they get round the difficulty :

(i) Either you are to blame or I am.
(ii) He is not ready, nor are you. Neither of you are ready.

Exercise 64.—Read the following sentences, selecting from the words in brackets the form of the pronoun that ought to be used :

1. Uncle Robert took David and — to the fair (I, me).
2. Is it George ? Yes it's —, sure enough (he, him).
3. Mary and — are camping together this summer (she, her). 4. — Devon lads are made of tough material (we, us). 5. The money was divided between Harold and — (I, me). 6. The Robinsons, Smiths and — always go touring together (they, them). 7. Let John and — do it (I, me). 8. You and — make good friends (he, him).

Exercise 65.—Rewrite the following sentences, avoiding ambiguity and unpleasant repetition :

1. The manager told his friend that he was ruined.
2. Whenever the Sealyham met the little Cairn, he wagged his tail with delight. 3. She quarrelled regularly with her sister, and she returned her sarcasm with direct affronts.

4. The doctor told the patient that his cure lay in his hands. 5. The vicar told the curate that he was an excellent preacher.

Exercise 66.—Rewrite the following sentences correctly :

1. John and you are representing the town. 2. She and you have never got on well together. 3. The Jacksons and you are the oldest members of the Club. 4. Mr. and Mrs. Holroyd and we have very little in common. 5. The children and you had better go first. 6. Me and him are used to roughing it. 7. Who is that knocking at my door ? Me, sir. 8. There is only Tom and Betty here so far. 9. Either she or I is wrong. 10. Neither Tom nor you are coming with me.

IV. Possessive Pronouns

The genitive or possessive case of the personal pronoun is sometimes called a *Possessive Pronoun*. The possessive case, like the accusative of the personal pronoun, is indicated by an inflexion :

I, me   mine
thou, thee   thine

Such possessive pronouns really mean *of me, of thee.* It must be remembered that *no apostrophe is used to denote the possessive case in pronouns* : e.g. That book is Mary's, but That book is *hers, yours, theirs.* Note specially *it's*—it is, and *its,* the possessive.

Exercise 67.—Rewrite the following passages, inserting the apostrophe where you think it is necessary :

1. Its a long lane that has no turning. 2. Is the book yours or mine ? 3. Jane is writing an article on womens fashions ; hers is about dress reform. 4. Theres not a shadow of doubt about it. 5. Theirs is a very different task.

V. Other Pronouns : Demonstrative, Interrogative, Indefinite

Read the following passage :

" This is the Old Castle," stated the guide, " and these are the walls that have confined many a prisoner." " What is that strange thing there?" asked one visitor, pointing to a strange wooden frame at the far end of the courtyard. "Those are the stocks," he replied, "where rebellious prisoners were placed till they learned how to behave. Anyone who kicked over the traces sampled them sooner or later. The gaolers gave each his turn."

(a) *This* is the old castle. *These* are the walls. *Those* are the stocks. The words *this*, *these* and *those* are doing the work of nouns; they are called *Demonstrative Pronouns* (Latin: *demonstrare*—point out). *This* and *these* point out things that are near to the speaker. *That* and *those* refer to things further away.

The Cockney is often heard emphasising the distinction between *this* and *that*. "This here is my cap; that there is yours."

(b) *What* is that thing? *What* is used instead of a noun. It is a pronoun, it introduces a question and is therefore an *Interrogative Pronoun*.

(c) *Anyone* samples them. *Anyone* is a pronoun which indicates some person or thing without particularising. It is called an *Indefinite Pronoun*. Note also *anybody*, *anything*, *someone*, *one*.

(d) The gaoler gave *each* his turn. *Each*, *everyone*, *either*, *neither* are called *Distributive Pronouns*, as they have a distinguishing or separating sense. Distributive pronouns are followed by verbs in the singular.

Exercise 68.—Fill in the blanks with suitable demonstrative pronouns:

1. "— is a wonderful bargain," said the salesman, holding up a yellow-metalled watch, "solid gold, going for 17s. 6d." 2. — was the finest holiday I have ever had. 3. — was your moment of triumph. — is your moment of humiliation. 4. "— are sad days," said the speaker, "but — to come will be brighter." 5. "— gives a very poor light," he said, as he switched on my torch, "— looks a better one."

Exercise 69.—Supply from the following list the interrogative pronoun most suitable in the following sentences (who, whom, which, what) :

1. — stands without ?   2. — is your name ?   3. — is your errand ?   4. — is the way to the tower ?   5. — will be the first ?   6. — are you recommending to be captain ?   7. For — are you voting ?   8. — do you think I am ?

Exercise 70.—Supply the correct number of the verb in the present tense after the following distributive adjectives :

1. Each — about his own business.   2. Everyone — his best.   3. Either of the ponies — a good mount.   4. Neither of the saddles — comfortable.

VI. Emphasising and Reflexive Pronouns

Examine the sentences :

1. Captain Bloater himself shot the first rabbit.
2. Captain Bloater shot himself.

What is *himself* doing in sentence 1 ?   It is emphasising the fact that Captain Bloater, and no one else, shot the first rabbit.   Now consider sentence 2.   The subject is *Captain Bloater*, the verb is *shot*, the object is *himself*. Thus the pronoun *himself* is the object of the transitive verb and refers back to the same person as the subject. It *reflects* the subject and is called a *Reflexive Pronoun*. Reflexive pronouns are the same in form as the emphasising pronouns.

> *Query :* What case is *himself* in sentence 1 : nominative or accusative ?   What case is it in sentence 2 ?

Exercise 71.—Say which pronouns are emphasising and which reflexive in the following :

1. I shall see the Mayor myself.   2. The Mayor himself will lead the procession.   3. She fancies herself in her new fur coat.   4. Would you do a thing like that yourself ? 5. They call themselves the " Young England Club." 6. Go yourself, you lazy beggar.   7. Look after yourself.

Exercise 72.—Pick out the pronouns in the following sentences, and state the kind :

We had now been in the maze for over three hours. One of the party had been looked upon as guide, but he was lost himself and we were lost with him. He had given each of us instructions to keep close to him. This we did most faithfully, but if ever there was a false guide, it was ours that day. We took this turning, we took that; if somebody remarked that we had passed that way before, we turned about and went the other. We reproached ourselves that anyone had tempted us ever to try the maze.

VII. Relative Pronouns

(i) Examine the following :

   1. (a) The thief was a very clever rogue. (b) He had twice eluded the police.

   2. The thief was a very clever rogue and twice he had eluded the police.

   3. The thief who had twice eluded the police was a very clever rogue.

Consider the word *who*. In sentence 3 it is used instead of the words *and he*. It is really doing the work of the two words *and* and *he*: (1) *and*, thus joining the two sentences 1 (a) and 1 (b) together ; (2) *he* is a personal pronoun. Thus in sentence 3, *who* relates one clause in the sentence to another and is a pronoun. It is called a *Relative Pronoun*.

Consider also :

   4. (a) I saw the church tower. (b) It was undamaged in spite of the fire. (c) I saw the church tower *which* was undamaged in spite of the fire.

   5. (a) This is the house. (b) Jack built it. (c) This is the house *that* Jack built.

Who, which, that are relative pronouns.

In sentence 4 (c), *which* relates back to *church tower*, and in sentence 5 (c), *that* relates back to *house*. The words *church tower* and *house* are said to be antecedents of the relative pronouns.

(ii) Consider the following :

   6. (a) Mrs. Chatters is the village busybody. (b) Nobody likes her.

7. Mrs. Chatters is the village busybody and nobody likes her.
8. Mrs. Chatters, whom nobody likes, is the village busybody.

Whom in sentence 8 is doing the work of *and* and the work of *her*, the object of the verb *like*. *Whom*, therefore, is the relative pronoun. *Which* and *that* are also found as the object of the verb, but the nominative and accusative forms are the same : e.g. (i) The business *which* had been in the family many years was soon bankrupt in his hands (nominative case, subject of verb *had been*). (ii) The house *which* he bought was of Edwardian architecture (accusative case, object of verb *had bought*).

N.B.—It is a very common practice to omit the relative pronoun when it is the object of the verb : e.g. *The house he bought was of Edwardian architecture* is as common as " The house *which* he bought."

VIII. Relative Clauses

It will be noted that the relative pronoun is used to introduce an adjectival clause : e.g. *whom nobody likes*, *which he bought*. These clauses are sometimes referred to as Relative Clauses.

Exercise 73.—Join the following pairs of sentences by the use of a relative pronoun. State the antecedent and the case of the relative pronoun (e.g. I know the man. You are employing. I know the man *whom* you are employing. (Ante. man. Accusative) :

1. It was an even game. It was watched by a crowd of spectators. 2. The home team wore white. They had the advantage of the presence of their own supporters. 3. The visiting side wore colours. They had travelled overnight from the North. 4. The referee was kept very busy. He was the object of many remarks, not always courteous, from the crowd. 5. The captain of the home team was a tower of strength to his side. The local supporters constantly cheered him. 6. The referee gave a penalty for offside against the home team. The right back took it.

Exercise 74.—State whether *who* or *whom* should be used in the following :

1. The man — stole the handbag was arrested at Bayswater. 2. It is a pleasure to meet old friends — one has not seen for so long. 3. The last man in the world — I expected to meet was on the quay to welcome us. 4. Have you seen the man — is the new tenant at " Chez-Nous " ? 5. I must call to see the town councillor — we want to open our bazaar. 6. The men — are employed in that factory work long hours.

Exercise 75.—Combine the parts of each group into single sentences, using *who*, *whom*, *which* or *that* to avoid a succession of short jerky sentences :

1. Mrs. Major Robertson was a woman of slight build. She had great beauty, energy, courage and sense. 2. One night she went to her bedroom. It was at the top of the house. 3. She left downstairs a young watchman. He was the only other occupant of the house. 4. Entering her bedroom she saw a portion of a man's foot. It was projecting from under the bed. 5. She gave no cry of alarm. It would have disturbed the thief. She began to undress. 6. Suddenly she stamped her foot. She addressed herself aloud in these words. The burglar could hear them. 7. " There, I've forgotten the key. I'm always leaving it downstairs." 8. Leaving the candle burning and the door open, she went down to the young watchman. He listened to her story. He returned to the bedroom with her. 9. The watchman secured the proprietor of the foot. It had not moved an inch. 10. How many women are there like this ? Could many show such cool common sense ?

Exercise 76.—Point out the adjectival clauses in the following sentences, stating the relative pronouns that have been omitted :

1. The house we rented was infested by rats. 2. The man you want is lodging at " The Pig and Glue-Pot." 3. The game I like best is tennis. 4. When you have read the book, pass it on to anyone you like. 5. The noise the car made caused everyone to turn round. 6. The girl I am courting told me I had the most unusual face she had ever seen.

c *

IX. Relative Pronouns used with Prepositions

1. Examine the sentences :

The man is a successful stock-broker.   I am working for him.

The man for *whom* I am working is a successful stock-broker.

Him is in the accusative because it is governed by a preposition.   (For fuller discussion cf. p. 88.)   In the combined sentence *whom* is a relative pronoun in the accusative case governed by *for*.

2. The possessive form of the relative pronoun may be used in respect of persons instead *of whom*.

e.g. The man *whose* shop was destroyed by fire was not insured.

The form *whose* is confined usually to persons, but sometimes it is found in reference to things : e.g. The moon *whose* light had at first been a boon to us was now a danger to our enterprise.

The Relative Adverb.—The relative adverb is often preferred to the combination of a *preposition and relative pronoun* as being simpler and more direct.

The room where (in which) I spent the night was cold and draughty.

The reason why I refused . . . (for which).

Exercise 77.—Complete adjectival clauses with the following sentences (e.g. The profession for which . . . (he was trained) was the law) :

1. The town in which . . . is situated on the river.
2. The methods by which . . . are not above suspicion.
3. She is not a woman for whom . . .   4. The girl whose hand . . . was an old friend of mine.   5. The soldier by whose . . . . slipped away unobserved.

X.

As is used also as a relative pronoun after *such, same* and repeated after *as* :

e.g. (i) She wore the same hat *as* she wore at her brother's wedding.

    (ii) Such a scene met my eyes *as* I never wish to see again.

    (iii) He was carrying as large a hare *as* I have seen for many a long day.

In these sentences *as* is introducing an adjectival clause qualifying in (i) *hat*, in (ii) *scene*, in (iii) *hare*.

Perhaps it should be noted here that relative adverbs also introduce adjectival clauses. You might say either : "I remember the house *in which* I was born"; or you might say : "I remember the house *where* I was born." *Which* is a *relative pronoun* governed by *in*. *Where* is a relative adverb introducing the adjectival clause. (Cf. p. 84.)

Exercise 78.—Complete the adjectival clauses in the following :

    1. This is the spot where . . . 2. After the War of 1914-1918 there followed a period when . . . 3. Can you give me the reason why . . . 4. The fox had gone to his home whence . . . 5. The Old Chief went to the Happy Hunting Ground whither . . .

Exercise 79.—Pick out the relative pronouns in the following and name the antecedents :

    1. The man who never made a mistake never made anything. 2. It's a long lane which hath no turning. 3. The actor whom you saw was an understudy. 4. I shall sing one of the songs that my mother used to sing. 5. Mr. Skinflint is as mean a man as you would find in a day's march. 6. He made the same jokes today as he made yesterday. 7. All that glitters is not gold. 8. The hotel where he usually stays is full.

XI. Pronouns and Adjectives

The same word may be used as an adjective or pronoun. It should not be difficult to distinguish between these two uses. An adjective is used in connection with a noun ; a pronoun is used *instead* of a noun :

    e.g. *This* is your opportunity (Demonstrative Pronoun).

This opportunity will never recur (Demonstrative Adjective).

The following table will illustrate the examples of words used as pronouns and adjectives :

Kind	*Pronoun*	*Adjective*
Possessive.	The money is *his*.	*His* hand held the tiller.
Demonstrative.	*Those* were great days.	*Those* men are dangerous.
Interrogative.	*What* are you doing ?	*What* seeds are you sowing ?
Indefinite.	*One* whispered to *another*.	*One* man might choose *another* topic.
Distributive.	*Each* is qualified for the post.	*Each* boy received five shillings.
Reflexive.	He disgraced *himself*.	(No use.)
Emphasising.	The Mayor *himself* took the chair.	„ „
Relative.	The story *which* he told me was incredible.	His account of his encounter with the law, *which* story no one believed, had been too often heard.

Exercise 80.—Construct sentences using the following as (i) Pronouns ; (ii) Adjectives :

these, thine, which ?, any, either, every, what, whatever, such.

XII. Parsing the Pronoun

When the pronoun is parsed, it is necessary to state : (i) The kind. (ii) Number. (iii) Person. (iv, Gender. (v) Case. (vi) Reason for its being in the case.

Exercise 81. — Parse the pronouns in the following sentences :

1. " I go a-milking, sir," she said. 2. Who will o'er the downs so free ? 3. Has anyone here seen Herbert ? 4. England will decline to fall, that's certain. 5. Such were some of you. 6. I chose the subject on which I had given much attention. 7. Let each go his own way. 8. He what prigs what isn't hisn, When he's copped he'll go to pris'n. 9. Go and fetch it yourself. 10. She fancies herself in her new fur coat.

Revision

1. What do you understand by : relative pronoun, relative clause, relative adverb ?

2. Below are some famous quotations. The pronoun in each appears in italics. State to whom the pronoun refers.

(i) *He* driveth furiously.

(ii) Am *I* my brother's keeper?

(iii) Male and female created He *them*.

(iv) *We* have seen his star in the East.

(v) This night, before the cock crow, *thou* shalt deny me thrice.

(vi) It had been good for that man if *he* had not been born.

3. State the *kind* of each of the pronouns in these quotations.

4. Write out six famous quotations containing a relative clause introduced by a relative pronoun (e.g. I have found my sheep *which was lost*).

5. In the following sentences, state whether the italicised word is an adjective or a pronoun :

(i) Physician, heal *thyself*.

(ii) What shall it profit a man, if he shall gain the whole world and lose *his own* soul ?

(iii) *Whose* fan is in *His* hand.

(iv) He hath put down the mighty from *their* seats and hath exalted *them* of low degree.

(v) *Thou* fool, *this* night *thy* soul shall be required of *thee*.

(vi) He *that* is faithful in *that which* is *least* is faithful also in *much*.

6. Define the following terms, giving an example of each. Check up your answers by reference to the appropriate chapter :

Present perfect tense, passive voice, nominative absolute, superlative degree, distributive pronoun.

CHAPTER VI

THE ADVERB

I. Adverbs of Manner, Time and Place

If you think you may be late for your train, you *walk briskly* to the station ; the thief *walks stealthily* along the dark street ; the farm-hand with a load of hay on his back *walks laboriously* ; the man emerging from the inn, it is feared, might *walk unsteadily*. Each of the words *briskly, stealthily, laboriously, unsteadily*, add to the meaning of the verb *walk*. They are called *Adverbs*. They add to the meaning of the verb by telling us how the action denoted by the verb is done. They show the *manner* in which the action is performed and are called *Adverbs of Manner*. You could supply many more adverbs of manner to the verb *walk*. The peacock would walk *proudly*, the loafer would walk *aimlessly*, and so on.

As an adverb of manner might be said to answer the question *how* ? (e.g. How did he walk ? He walked *briskly*), an adverb of time would answer the question *when* ? (e.g. *Yesterday* we walked over the common. We have walked twelve miles *today*), and an *adverb of place* would answer the question *where* ? (e.g. We shall walk *there*. *Here* comes the bride).

Exercise 82.—Supply adverbs of manner in the following (e.g. The tramp ate the meal — (*ravenously*)) :

1. The miser counted his gold —. 2. The speaker apologised — for being so late. 3. The sheep were bleating — in the cold blast. 4. Did you sleep — last night ? 5. I was — rewarded for my work.

Exercise 83.—Supply six adverbs that could be used with each of the following verbs (e.g. speak *kindly, harshly softly, loudly vehemently, eloquently*) :

behave, write, dress, work, eat.

Exercise 84.—In each of the following sentences supply a more picturesque adverb than the one given :

1. The prisoner answered the questions *well*. 2. She has learnt to behave *nicely*. 3. How *badly* she walks ! 4. In spite of all his money he speaks *awfully*. 5. That young man eats his food *terribly*.

Exercise 85.—Supply suitable adverbs of time in the following (e.g. The Smiths returned from their holiday — (*today*)) :

1. The dawn will — break. 2. The moment for striking has — come. 3. — we lost, today we will win. 4. I am taking the Intermediate this year, — I shall take my finals. 5. —, the fire was burning furiously.

Exercise 86.—Supply suitable adverbs of place in the following (e.g. I live — (*here*)):

1. — go the ships. 2. He is a much-travelled man, he has been —. 3. — I stand, I can none other. 4. " I lives —," said the old man, pointing to the cottage on the other side of the valley. 5. The inn sign was swaying — and — in the wind.

II. Adverb Equivalents

(i) *The adjective* is sometimes used as an equivalent of the adverb : e.g. The sun shines *bright* ; but the use is rare and is limited almost entirely to poetic language. The appearance of the adjective in the place of the adverb in such slovenly expressions as the following is far from poetic : *Hurry back*, QUICK. *She sang* BEAUTIFUL. *He treated me* HANDSOME.

(ii) " *Bang* goes sixpence," said MacTavish. *Bang* is usually a verb : here it is used adverbially. Thus *verbs* may be used as adverbs.

(iii) *Nouns* may be used as adverbs : e.g. I go rolling *home*.

(iv) Phrases can sometimes express the manner of the action of a verb more fully than a single word : e.g. You'll look sweet *upon the seat of a bicycle made for two* (place). He won the prize *by fair means* (manner). I'll meet you *in the morning* (time).

(v) *Clauses* may do the work of an adverb : e.g. (*a*) We dare not advance *yet*.   We dare not advance *until we receive orders* (time).   (*b*) You will find primroses *everywhere*.   *You* will find primroses *wherever you look* (place).   (*c*) The Tribunal dealt with the case *fairly*.   The Tribunal dealt with the case *as it deserved* (manner).

Exercise 87.—Point out the adverbs, adverbial phrases and adverbial clauses in the following passage. State whether they denote manner, place or time.

" Pleasure Party Rate "

They stood solemnly outside the booking office ; each member of the party was dressed in heavy black ; each held in his hand a wreath.   The leader of the little company then approached the ticket window.   As he advanced, the rest followed him.   Their clothes, their faces, their wreaths instantly betrayed their destination ; their speech equally betrayed their origin.   " Eight cheap returns to Perth," asked the leader in a gloomy voice, as he handed his wreath to his neighbour whilst his hand went to his pocket. " Eight ? " queried the official after he peered through the window at the dour faces.   " Yes, eight ! " came the doleful reply. " Pleasure party."

Exercise 88.—Correct the following sentences by re-arranging misplaced adverbial equivalents :

1. You will see that no one has lived in this house for years with half an eye.   2. The organist played a voluntary whilst the rector entered with much feeling.   3. The audience gave the speaker a loud cheer when he sat down. 4. Ladies are generally speaking as he indicated.   5. He should have given the electorate greater opportunities of seeing him in my view.

III. Other Kinds of Adverbs

1. *Adverbs of Degree.*—These are very common in English : e.g. The car travelled *rather, quite, fairly, very, exceedingly* fast.

The words in italics indicate the *degree* of the travelling fast.   Adverbs of degree may qualify adjectives and adverbs : e.g. (i) It was an *exceptionally* hot day. (ii) He did *exceptionally* well in his last examination.

Modern English has seen the introduction of a considerable number of adverbs of degree ; some of them have come in and out of fashion ; others of them are overworked and become monotonous. Some, however, are very expressive. We all get weary of the young lady who peppers her conversation with *awfully* or *perfectly* ; or of the young gentleman who peppers his thus : " a d— funny business," " he writes d— badly." These are indications of a limited vocabulary. But " up to my eyes in work," " head over heels in love," give a good picture.

Exercise 89.—Suggest alternatives for the following adverbs and adverbial equivalents :

1. A *jolly* bad headache. 2. He bullies me *something awful*. 3. He went *off the deep end* at me. 4. She looks *frightfully* smart. 5. How *terribly* kind of you. 6. I'm broke *to the wide*.

2. *Interrogative Adverbs.*—Consider the sentences :

    (i) *When* are you taking up your new post ?
    (ii) *Where* is your coat ?

The words *when* and *where* are adverbs introducing questions and are called Interrogative Adverbs. Adverbial equivalents might also be used : e.g. *On what date* are you taking up your new post ? *On which peg* is your coat ? These interrogative adverbs and equivalents indicate time and place.

Similarly, an interrogative adverb or its equivalent may introduce a question referring to manner (e.g. how ?) and to reason (e.g. why ?).

Exercise 90.—Suggest three adverbial phrases that could introduce a question referring to time, place, manner, reason (e.g. On what day ? On which post ? In what way ? For what purpose ?).

3. *Adverbs of Affirmation and Negation and their Equivalents.*—Consider these sentences :

    (i) You will *certainly* fail. (ii) I know *not* the man.

Certainly affirms the verb *will fail*. *Not* represents a denial. *Certainly* is an adverb of *affirmation*. *Not* is an adverb of *negation*.

Affirmation and negation may be indicated by an adverbial equivalent : e.g. You will fail *beyond a shadow of doubt*. He can *by no means* succeed.

In this connection we must examine the most used words in the English language : *Yes* and *No*.

Examine the following :

JACK. Do you love me ?   JILL. Yes. (The reader may add appropriate terms of endearment, according to taste.)

JACK. Will you marry me then ?   JILL. No.

The words *Yes* and *No* are often called adverbs because they seem to be more like adverbs than any other part of speech. But are they true adverbs ? What would be the equivalent answer to Jack's first question, *Do you love me ?* It would be, *I do love you*. To his second question, *Will you marry me ?* the sad reply would be, *I shall not marry you*. The words *Yes* and *No* are therefore in these sentences equivalents, and perhaps they should be called *Sentence-Words* ; it is a long name for short words.

Exercise 91.—State the part of speech of the words italicised in the following sentences :

1. Are you there ? *Yes.* 2. Is Tom with you ? *No.* 3. Believest thou this ? *Yea*, Lord. 4. *Yea*, though I walk through the valley of death. 5. I have *no* hope save thine. 6. *No* small sum. 7. His reply was, " *Yes.*" 8. *Aye, aye*, cap'n. 9. *Yes*, you are right. 10. The *Noes* have it.

Exercise 92.—Form adverbs from the following :

(a) *Adjectives* : smooth, moody, dramatic, callous, majestic, gay, good, fast.

(b) *Nouns* : moment, hour, day, sleep, length, time, heaven, side, shore.

Exercise 93.—(i) Can you think of any adjectives ending in *-ly* : e.g. stately ? (ii) Can you form adverbs from them ? (iii) Give other instances of words where adverb formation is different.

Exercise 94.—Which of the words italicised in the following sentences are adjectives and which are adverbs ?

1. The *fast* driver meets with trouble one day. 2. Don't go so *fast*. 3. Uncle Remus is a *late* caller. 4. I arrived *late* at the club. 5. She moves with *queenly* grace. 6. He smiled *serenely*. 7. Our *daily* bread. 8. The bread is delivered *daily*. 9. The natives appear *unfriendly*. 10. Your coming is *timely*. 11. The night was *still*. 12. The enemy is *still* retreating.

4. *Comparison of Adverbs.*—(i) Adverbs can be compared in the same way as adjectives :

e.g. Jack runs *fast*. Mary writes *carefully*. (Positive.)
George runs *faster*. Joan writes *more carefully*. (Comparative.)
The trainer runs *fastest*. Peggy writes *most carefully*. (Superlative.)

(ii) Some of the comparisons are irregular : e.g. Harry works *well* ; Arthur works *better* ; Robert works *best*. Also, *little, less, least ; much, more, most.*

(iii) Some adverbs have the same comparative and superlative forms as their corresponding adjectives :

good	better	best	(Adjective)
well	better	best	(Adverb)
bad	worse	worst	(Adjective)
badly	worse	worst	(Adverb)

Exercise 95.—Write the comparative degree of the following adverbs :

soon, tenderly, most, last, often, next, ill, furthest, fast.

IV. Position of the Adverb

Consider the sentences :

1. Only the Bloomsbury-Burtons hired two cars for the party.
2. The Bloomsbury-Burtons only hired two cars for the party.

3. The Bloomsbury-Burtons hired only two cars **for** the party.

4. The Bloomsbury-Burtons hired two cars only for the party.

Only occupies a different position in each sentence. What difference of meaning is conveyed by the different position of *only* ?

The adverb, then, is usually placed close to the word it qualifies. If the meaning of the sentence would be unaffected and the balance of the sentence improved, there is no reason to condemn the practice in colloquial speech of its being at another place in the sentence. Thus most people would say : *He only came yesterday.* The meaning is clear enough, but the precisionist would prefer : *He came only yesterday.*

Exercise 96.—Comment on the correctness or otherwise of the following sentences :

1. He merely visits our family for what he can get out of us.

2. England will only remain a great world power as long as she keeps her sea-communication open.

3. Young Charles only joined the club last week. Now he wants to run it.

4. Mary only asked the porter to carry her bag.

Exercise 97.—Substitute antonyms for the adverbs italicised in the following sentences (e.g. She walks gracefully. She walks clumsily) :

1. He spoke *haltingly*. 2. He *willingly* agreed to our plan. 3. He swung the axe *carefully*. 4. It rained *continuously*. 5. Our wireless *often* fails. 6. He recounted his experiences *proudly*.

V. Relative Adverbs

Consider the sentence :

The inn at which we stayed used to be one of the old post houses.

Instead of the phrase *at which*, made up of a preposition

and relative pronoun, the relative adverb *where* could be used :

The inn *where* we stayed . . .

Exercise 98.—Construct sentences, using the following words as relative adverbs : when, where, how, why (e.g. The year when the Normans invaded England was 1066).

VI. Parsing the Adverb

In parsing the adverb, state :

(i) The kind. (ii) The degree, if it can be compared. (iii) The word it qualifies.

Exercise 99.—(*a*) Parse the adverbs in the following :

1. Too many cooks spoil the broth. 2. It never rains but it pours. 3. He laughs best who laughs last. 4. Well begun is half done. 5. Once bitten, twice shy. 6. Least said, soonest mended.

    (*b*) Down dropt the breeze, the sails dropt down,
        'Twas sad as sad could be.
        And we did only speak to break
        The silence of the sea.

    (*c*) He lives long that lives well.

Exercise 100.—Use the group of words below in sentences : (i) as noun equivalents ; (ii) adjectival equivalents ; (iii) adverbial equivalents (e.g. When the stranger arrived. No one knew when the stranger arrived (noun). It was a misty day when the stranger arrived (adjective). When the stranger arrived, the conversation suddenly ceased (adverb)) :

1. Where do flies go in the winter-time ? 2. When my ship comes home. 3. Whither the birds fly. 4. Across the Atlantic. 5. Over the hill.

VII. Nominative Absolute

It might be noticed here that sometimes instead of an adverbial clause a construction is used composed of a noun or a pronoun together with a participle.

Consider the following :

  (i) When the game was over, the spectators went home.
  (ii) The game being over, the spectators went home.

In sentence (ii) a participial phrase is used for an adverbial clause. This participial phrase is called a Nominative Absolute. Cf. pp. 45-46.

Revision

1. What do you understand by the following :

  (i) Adverb of Degree ;
  (ii) Comparative Degree of the Adverb ;
  (iii) Interrogative Adverbs ?

2. Read the following and answer the questions below :

> One more unfortunate,
> Weary of breath,
> Rashly importunate,
> Gone to her death.
>
> Take her up tenderly.
> Lift her with care.
> Fashioned so slenderly,
> Young and so fair.

  (i) Pick out three adjectives of quality.
 (ii) Pick out two adverbs of manner, two adverbs of degree.
 (iii) Pick out one phrase used as adjectival equivalent.
 (iv) Pick out two phrases used as adverbial equivalents.

3. Analyse the two sentences in stanza 2 into subject and predicate.

4. Find synonyms and antonyms for the following. Use your dictionary if necessary :

  (i) *Nouns :* fear, health, greed, shame, arrival.
 (ii) *Verbs :* ask, defend, borrow, trust, command.
 (iii) *Adjectives :* ambitious, apt, talkative, urgent, discreet.
 (iv) *Adverbs :* fast, sternly, well, carefully, firstly.

CHAPTER VII

THE PREPOSITION

I.

Mr. Chestnut has a stall *near the Park*. Mr. Nougat has a stall *by the Park*. Mr. Creamo has a stall *in the Park*.

The words *near the Park, by the Park, in the Park,* are adjectival phrases describing *stall.* Each adds a different meaning to the word *stall*. The words *near, by, in* show the relationship between the *stalls* owned by the three vendors and the Park.

Each phrase is made up of a noun, the *Park*, and another word, *near, by, in*. These words are called *Prepositions*. A preposition is a word used with a noun or noun equivalent to show its relation with some other word in the sentence. The meaning of the word *preposition* is *placed before*. The preposition is most commonly placed before the noun or pronoun.

Exercise 101.—Supply suitable prepositions in adjectival phrases in the following (e.g. The house — the corner is to let (*at*)) :

1. The ships — the high seas met the full blast of the hurricane. 2. The men — the mine were in great danger. 3. The pilot — the aircraft realised something was wrong. 4. Kingston — Thames is situated — Surrey. 5. A sight — description met our eyes.

II.

Similarly, prepositions help to form adverbial phrases.

The cat scampered *up* a tree, *down* a tree, *across* the road, *along* the roof, *through* the window.

These are all adverbial phrases indicating place.

Exercise 102.—Supply suitable prepositions in the adverbial phrases in the following :

1. The policeman tramped — his beat. 2. The cow jumped — the moon. 3. The postman knocked — the

door. 4. The sun disappeared — the clouds. 5. The wind beat — the traveller's face. 6. The boy fell — his cycle.

Exercise 103.—Point out the prepositions showing the relationship between the noun or noun equivalent which follows and—

(*a*) A verb : 1. He writes for a living. 2. The bungalow is near the sea. 3. Don't dilly-dally by the way. 4. Just for a handful of silver he left us. 5. He has gone beyond recall.

(*b*) An adjective : 1. The Captain is proud of his achievement. 2. She is clever with the brush. 3. The grass was heavy with dew. 4. What are you good at ?

(*c*) A noun : 1. The building was a mass of ruins. 2. I found a hole in the wall. 3. We enjoyed the walk along the shore. 4. The house with the garage was sold for £2000. 5. Most folk enjoy a nap after dinner.

III. The Object of the Preposition

Consider the following :

A holiday *without him* would not be a holiday.
The mist gathered around *us*.

In the adjectival phrase *without him*, the preposition has affected the form of the pronoun. It is in the accusative or objective case. Similarly, in the adverbial phrase *around us*, the pronoun is in the accusative case. In English, the preposition governs the noun or noun equivalent in the accusative. There is no difference in form between a noun in the nominative and the same noun in the accusative case in English, but the form of the pronoun *does* change, *he* to *him*, *we* to *us*. But whether the accusative case is indicated in a change of form or not, the preposition governs the accusative case.

IV. Parsing the Preposition

In parsing the preposition, state the word that it governs :

Exercise 104.—Parse the prepositions in the following :

1. Drink to me only with thine eyes. 2. Who will o'er the downs with me ? 3. You'll look sweet upon the seat

of a bicycle made for two.   4. I'll be in Scotland before ye.
5. For whom, my heart, were all those sorrows borne?
6. From him I'll never, no, never depart.   7. Give to me
the life I love.   8. I vow to thee, my Country.   9. Up,
Guards, and at 'em.

10.   I went to the animals' fair,
       The beasts and the birds were there.
       The old baboon by the light of the moon
       Was combing his auburn hair.
       The monkey fell out of his bunk
       And slipped down the elephant's trunk.
       The elephant sneezed and fell on his knees,
       But what became of the monk-ey?

V. Correct Constructions

1. In pronouns where there is a difference in the form of
the nominative and accusative, care must be exercised that
a pronoun governed by a preposition is in the accusative
form.   Errors sometimes creep in when the preposition is
used to govern two pronouns or one noun and a pronoun:

e.g. As for Mary and me (not I), we are too tired for
     another set.

For governs *me* as well as *Mary*.

Exercise 105.—Supply the correct form of the pronoun
in the following:

1. The porter gave permission for Smith and — to visit
the royal suite (I, me).   2. There is enough here for you
and — (he, him).   3. Between you and —, that man does
not deserve your trust (I, me).   4. She had given up everything for her brother, — who now scorned her (he, him).
5. It is for — young people to be the architects of the
future (we, us).   6. With — are you travelling? (who,
whom).   7. Nobody but you and — saw him go (she, her).
8. — the dickens do you think you are talking to? (who,
whom).

2. Certain prepositions are always used with certain
words.   As is not uncommon in the English language, no
definite rules can be given which are applicable to all

words, but as the reader meets special combinations of word and preposition in his reading he should note them.

Here are a few examples :

> *Nouns :* grudge against, freedom from, enmity with, authority on/over, identity with.
>
> *Adjectives :* similar to, conscious of, different from, typical of, synonymous with.
>
> *Verbs :* prevail against, prevent from, acquiesce with, agree to a thing, agree with a person, compensate for.

Exercise 106.—Construct sentences containing the following words followed by appropriate prepositions :

(a) *Nouns :* (1) parody, (2) thirst, (3) suspicion, (4) jurisdiction, (5) bias, (6) heir.

(b) *Adjectives :* (1) full, (2) opposite, (3) dependent, (4) contemporary, (5) averse, (6) analogous.

(c) *Verbs :* (1) digress, (2) approve, (3) vie, (4) derive, (5) delve, (6) inveigh.

Exercise 107.—Insert the right preposition in the following sentences :

1. Sheila has a taste — poetry.   2. This cheese tastes — paraffin.   3. I correspond — a cousin in Canada.   4. This piece corresponds — that.   5. The professor is an authority — early printed books.   6. The King exercises authority — millions of subjects.   7. He has a degree — common sense.   8. He has a degree — classics.   9. Have you been — your study all the morning ?   10. I have not been — my study yet this morning.   11. There came a big spider, And sat down — her.   12. There were five thousand men — women and children.   13. The river runs — two ranges of hills.   14. Divide this — John, Mary and Jane.   15. Shakespeare was born — Stratford-on-Avon — the county of Warwickshire.

3. "Never use a preposition to end a sentence with." So runs the schoolmaster's tag. Perhaps in formal written English his advice should be followed as far as possible. There are occasions, especially in conversational English, when the preposition can quite justifiably appear at the end of the sentence. Many verbs in our language are commonly used in close connection with prepositions such

as : to put on (clothes) ; to grumble at ; to work for, etc.
For instance, which is preferable :

>   This is a job to be jumped at.
>   This is a job at which to jump ;

or again :

>   I have a case to put my tools in ; or,
>   I have a case in which to put my tools ?

4. *To/For and Accusative.*—We have already discussed
the use of the dative in English for the Indirect Object.

>   The Mayor gave *me* the prize.

>   Direct Object :   prize.
>   Indirect Object :   *me*.
>   *me* is dative case.

The meaning is the same but the construction is different
if the sentence is written :

>   The Mayor gave the prize to me.

>   Direct Object :   prize.
>   Adverbial Phrase :   to me.

me is accusative case governed by preposition *to*.

5. *Some Mistaken Uses of Prepositions.*—(i) *Between* (by-
twain) can refer to two things only. If three or more are
indicated, *among*, *amongst* must be used :

e.g. Divide the apple between the two of you.

>   The country was shared amongst the Angles, the
>   Saxons and the Jutes.

(ii) *But* is normally a conjunction (see Chapter VIII),
but when it is used as a preposition it must govern the
accusative :

>   Don't sit under the apple-tree
>   With anyone else but *me*.

Yet in the Book of Common Prayer we find :

" There is none other that fighteth for us, but only
Thou, O Lord ! "

There is an implied contraction here : " There is none
other that fighteth for us, but only Thou fightest for us."

N.B.—Note the use of *but* as a relative pronoun with a negative case.

> There was no one present but (who not) did recognise the young pianist's talent.

(iii) *Like* is often used as a preposition :

> Mary is *like* me : she prefers hockey to dancing.

Like is *never* used as a conjunction :

> Arthur is a busybody *like* his sister used to be.

For *like* read *as*, which can be used as a conjunction.

(iv) Confusion of preposition.

Consider the following :

> (i) It is *on* the House of Commons that the country looks for leadership in the work of reconstruction.

The inversion of order has caused the wrong preposition to be used. For *on* read *to*. Or, alternatively, change the verb *looks* to *relies*.

> (ii) *To* a person of your experience the task of reorganisation of the business will come as no difficult matter *to* you.

In this sentence the preposition *to* has been unnecessarily repeated. Omit *to you*.

These incorrect uses of prepositions arise through carelessness and can be avoided by a little thought.

Exercise 108.—Insert *past* (a preposition) or *passed* (a verb) in the following :

1. The coach drove — my window. 2. —, present and future. 3. She swept right — me. 4. The player — the ball to the goalie. 5. It is half — five. 6. Poor old Mellar has — away.

Exercise 109.—State whether the words italicised in the following sentences are adverbs or prepositions :

1. Jack and Jill went *up* the hill. 2. Get *up*, you lazy beggar. 3. " Come *in*," cried the Mayor, looking bigger, And *in* did come the strangest figure. 4. *Underneath* the spreading chestnut tree. 5. *Underneath* were six beautiful eggs. 6. Coming *through* the rye. 7. Two eyes of blue

are smiling *through*.   8. The horse has fallen *over*.   9. *Over* the fence jumped Sonny Jim.   10. *In* you go, little chicks.

Exercise 110.—What part of speech are the words italicised in :

> When I am *out*, my scorer,
> Write no sad thoughts for me ;
> And if I score a fourer,
> Oh, write not *down* a three.
> And if I fail to get one,
> *To* me some other's set,
> *Thus*, if I score, remember,
> And if I don't, forget.

Exercise 111.—Correct the following sentences :

1. The new scheme is contrary to the plans previously recommended by the sub-committee and with what was urged by the Regional Commissioner.

2. The gold was shared between the pirate captain, the mate and the ship's cook.

3. To me the thought of the destruction of those historic works of art gives me great pain.

4. The boy stood on the burning deck whence all but he had fled.

5. This camera is different to yours in many ways. My snaps are not satisfactory like yours always are.

6. What do you want to be read to for ?

7. Poverty with happiness is more preferable than wealth with sorrow.

Revision

1. What do you understand by :
   (i) a participial phrase ;
   (ii) a prepositional phrase ?

2. Pick out (*a*) the prepositions, (*b*) the interjections in the following passages :

> (i)   He said, " I look for butterflies
> That sleep among the wheat :
> I make them into mutton-pies,
> And sell them in the street."   LEWIS CARROLL.

(ii)   Of all the days that's in the week
       I dearly love but one day,
       And that's the day that comes betwixt
       A Saturday and Monday.

CAREY.

(iii) Alas, master, for it was borrowed.

(iv) Ugh ! it was a ghastly experience.

3. What prepositions usually follow the following ?

different, prefer, contact, expert, hostile, dealer, accessory.

4. (a) Show how the verb *act* has a different meaning as it is followed by the adverbs *in*, *for*, *by*.

(b) How many meanings can you give to the word *put* by associating it with different prepositions ?

5. Construct sentences using the word *down* as : noun, adjective, verb, adverb, preposition.

CHAPTER VIII

THE CONJUNCTION AND INTERJECTION

I. THE CONJUNCTION

(a) A railway junction is a place where two lines of rails *join*. It is necessary sometimes to have a junction between words : e.g. pork *and* greens, sausage *and* mash, hop *and* skip, slowly *but* surely, *neither* here *nor* there. Can you suggest other commonly used doublets ?

The " junction " or joining words are called Conjunctions. They link not only words but phrases and sentences :

> e.g. (i) With a heavy heart *but* with a cheerful smile he faced his new task.
>
> (ii) We gathered up our luggage *and* left the compartment.

(b) Parsing the Conjunction

In parsing the conjunction, state what it is joining— words, phrases, clauses. If it is joining clauses, it may be either a co-ordinating or subordinating conjunction.

Exercise 112.—Note the italicised conjunctions in the following sentences. State whether they are joining words, phrases or sentences :

1. There's a cry *and* a shout, *and* a terrible rout,
   And nobody seems to know what they're about,
   But the Monks have their pockets all turned inside out.

2.   If all the world were paper,
         And all the sea were ink,
         And all the trees were bread *and* cheese,
         What should we do for drink ?

3.   Alone stood brave Horatius
         But constant still in mind.

4.   No sound of joy *or* sorrow
         Was heard from either bank.

5.   Look *before* you leap.

6. *As* Caesar loved me, I weep for him ; *as* he was fortunate, I rejoice at it ; *as* he was valiant, I honour him ; *but, as* he was ambitious, I slew him.

Exercise 113.—With the aid of conjunctions, join the following sentences. (It is possible to shift the emphasis of the combined sense according to your arrangement.)

1. Swallows migrate in winter. Robins stay during the whole year. 2. We reached the top of the hill. A glorious view lay before us. 3. The courts are under water. We cannot play tennis. 4. There is a hole under the floor boards. The mice get into the larder. There is a good stock of food. 5. I am looking forward to Christmas. I shall be leaving the town. I am going into the country. I am expecting a merry time.

Exercise 114.—Supply suitable conjunctions in the blank spaces :

1. Slowly — gently we laid him down. 2. The judge addressed him kindly — firmly. 3. He is honest — poor. 4. He is thirteen — fourteen years of age. 5. You may not go out — your work is done. 6. I had opened the door — he had time to knock. 7. — we were at the party, the house was burgled. 8. He told us — the factory was on fire.

Exercise 115.—Construct sentences using *either . . . or, neither . . . nor.*

(c) Correct Constructions

(i) *Scarcely . . . when.*

Consider the sentence :

Scarcely had the plane left the air-field when the starboard engine failed.

Notice *scarcely . . .* is followed by *when* and not by *than.*

(ii) *Try to.*

Try to buy me a copy of " Androcles and the Lion."

Notice *try to . . .* not *try and . . .*

Query : Is there any difference in meaning between *He was told to try to succeed* and *He was told to try and succeed* ?

(iii) *Like, except,* cannot be used as conjunctions : e.g. He works hard *as* (not *like*) his father did when he was young. The sentry will not admit you *unless* (not *except*) you are accompanied by one of the military.

(d) Conjunctions and Prepositions

Some words may be used both as conjunctions and prepositions :

e.g. The book lay open *before* me. (Preposition.)

Before the storm breaks, let us seek shelter. (Conjunction.)

Exercise 116.—State whether the italicised words are prepositions or conjunctions :

1. She is pretty *but* bad-tempered. 2. She thinks of nobody *but* herself. 3. *After* dinner, rest awhile. 4. *After* the investigation was completed, the inspector was in a position to make an arrest. 5. There has been no rain *since* St. Swithin's Day. 6. *Since* you insist on knowing, I am twenty-six years of age.

II. THE INTERJECTION

There are many occasions when we involuntarily express some sudden feeling or sentiment. As the dentist extracts an obstinate tooth, the patient draws in his breath, saying " Oh ! " " It's out ! " says the dentist with triumph, holding up the offending molar for inspection. The patient now breathes out and says " Ah ! "

Such words are called *Interjections* because they are *thrown among* other words in a sentence to express an emotion. They give the speaker or writer an opportunity to express his own feelings. The interjection is followed by a mark of punctuation. It must be remembered that the interjection plays no part in the construction of the sentence.

Exercise 117.—What emotion is usually associated with the following interjections :

1. Hurrah ! 2. Bother ! 3. Pshaw ! 4. Ugh ! 5. Tut ! 6. Sh !

D

Exercise 118.—With what persons or places do you associate the following interjections :

1. Lo! 2. S'death! 3. Och aye! 4. Indeed to goodness! 5. Achtung! 6. Attaboy! 7. Caramba! 8. Tiens! 9. Begorra! 10. Ba goom!

Exercise 119.—Construct sentences using interjections to express : fear, surprise, regret, reproof, love.

Revision

Study the following passages and answer the questions that follow.

1.
> Multiplication is vexation,
> Division is *as* bad.
> The Rule *of* Three *doth* puzzle me,
> *And* Practice drives me mad.

(a) Point out the nouns in the passage and state their case.

(b) What part of speech are the words in italics ?

2.
> *Three* wise men of Gotham
> Went to sea in a bowl.
> And if the bowl had been stronger,
> *My* song would have been *longer*.

(a) Analyse the first sentence into subject and predicate.

(b) Parse the italicised words.

3.
> As I *was going* to St. Ives,
> I met a man with seven wives,
> *Every* wife had seven sacks,
> Every sack had seven cats,
> Every cat had seven kits.
> Kits, cats, sacks and wives,
> How many were there going to St. Ives?

(a) Name the conjunctions and prepositions in this passage.

(b) Parse italicised words.

CHAPTER IX

A REVISION CHAPTER

I. Case

It will have been noted that during our consideration of the various parts of speech it has been necessary to refer to *case*. We have lost most endings in English in the noun (the exception is the 's in the genitive). Case, therefore, should be regarded not so much as a form but indicating a *relation*.

For instance :

> John always accompanied *her* on these journeys.

her is the accusative indicating a relation—it is the object of the transitive verb " accompanied."

With the exception of the vocative case, the cases that are used in English have already been referred to, but for revision purposes a table is appended with an example of a noun, *master*, and a pronoun *thou* :

	Singular		*Plural*
Nominative.	Master.	The master sat at his desk.	Masters.
	Thou.	Thou art the man.	You.
Vocative.	O Master.	O Master, save me.	O Masters.
	Thou.	Thou knave, thou hast fooled me.	You.
Accusative.	Master.	I hate my master.	Masters.
	Thee.	I love thee, sweet mistress.	You.
Genitive.	Master's.	There is my master's writing.	Masters'.
	Thy.	Thy Kingdom come.	Your.
Dative.	Master.	I gave the master my name.	Masters.
	Thee.	I will tell thee all.	You.

You will find in some books alternative names for the cases, as :

For Nominative :	Subjective Case.
Accusative :	Objective ,,
Genitive :	Possessive ,,
Dative :	Indirect Objective.

Exercise 120.—Write four sentences illustrating the use of the Nominative : (i) as subject of a sentence ; (ii) in apposition to a noun in nominative case ; (iii) as a complement ; (iv) in the nominative absolute.

Exercise 121.—Write five sentences illustrating the use of the Accusative : (i) as object of a transitive verb ; (ii) as cognate object ; (iii) as object of a preposition ; (iv) in apposition to a noun in accusative case ; (v) adverbially used : e.g. He ran three *miles*.

Exercise 122.—Write one sentence illustrating the use of the Dative Case to express indirect object.

Exercise 123.—Write two sentences illustrating the use of the Genitive Case : (i) in the singular ; (ii) in the plural.

II. Exercises on all the Parts of Speech

Exercise 124.—Comment on the grammar of the words in italics in the following :

1. Long *live* the King. 2. *Seeing* is believing. 3. *The weather being fine*, a picnic was arranged. 4. The dishonest fitter was given *notice*. 5. We had now walked *a mile*. 6. *What* an exciting day it was ! 7. *Crack* went the pistol. 8. That man has the wisdom of *Solomon*. 9. I bought it at *Selfridge's*. 10. She cut off their tails with a *carving* knife. 11. I gave him the book *myself*. 12. He is as good a man *as* ever came to Fairmile. 13. Nobody was there *but* gave him a cordial welcome. 14. The intrepid airman looped the *loop*. 15. The dressmaker has made *her* a most attractive dress. 16. It was a *contemptible* act. 17. We are bound to win *bar* accidents. 18. It is resolved that the next meeting *be called* on April 20th. 19. The ships *leave* port tonight. 20. You are a *walking* encyclopaedia. 21. Taffy was a *Welshman*. 22. He is a *somewhat* irascible young gentleman. 23. You have the *very* book I want. 24. We arose *betimes*. 25. Look *sharp* ! 26. *Milton !* Thou shouldst be living at this hour.

III. Correct Constructions

Exercise 125.—Rewrite the following sentences in a correct form :

1. Handwriting is rarely taught today unless to younger people. 2. Everyone of us have to bring our lunch and

tea with us. 3. He was the kind of man to constantly quarrel with honest folk like you and I. 4. I shall be pleased to accept your invitation for Saturday next. 5. Of these three schemes for the replanning of the town, the latter is the most ambitious. 6. In a large factory many matters for the welfare of the workers are often overlooked, which, if they were considered, the factory would be a happier place. 7. As I am lain up in bed with lumbago, you will excuse me refusing your kind invitation. 8. She is the most handsome of all her sisters and the most well-spoken member of the family. 9. One cannot help but feel sorry for the poor wretch. 10. Let Mary and I determine here and now, that nobody but he is appointed captain. 11. He said that if he had to make a choice between a light post in which he had little responsibility or a heavy one in which he had heavy responsibility, he would choose the latter. 12. I have entered for the competition, but I do not think I will win a prize. 13. This seems the longest night of all others that we have endured. 14. The analysis of the sentences were poorly done by most candidates. 15. This was hardly the occasion to exalt over his successes. 16. Being co-directors, the issue had to be decided upon between the three men. 17. Who would you most prefer to work with ? 18. It was him that the blow was aimed at. 19. My son has now reached the top of the tree, and it is now all plain sailing. 20. Mr. Abelwhite presents his complements to Mr. Spiffin and begs to say I shall not be able to give you a game of golf on Monday as I have an attack of gout. 21. We are all very sorry to miss the vacant face of our President at our opening meeting. 22. The poor fellow who was knocked down by a heavy lorry was taken to the Northbridge Hospital, where he has since died in an unconscious condition. 23. He only comes to see me when he wants to borrow something off of me. 24. The story of the " Mayor of Casterbridge " centres round the character of Michael Henchard. 25. While walking through the fields with my friend, a bull suddenly attacked us. 26. Surely one can behave as one likes in his own home. 27. Dogsley is the man whom we hoped would be elected to Parliament. 28. Are either of these girls more perfect at their work than me ?   29. Nobody but I and you need know the real circumstances what led to his dismissal.   30. The pamphlet was written to incite public opinion against a man whom you know is a worthy citizen.

Revision

1. Explain the meaning of :
   Understood Subject.
   Indirect Object.
   Nominative of Address.
   Adverbial Accusative.
   Cognate Object.

2. Show the ways in which the Possessive is indicated in English.

3. Comment on the case of the italicised words in the following :

   (i) It's *me*, O Lord,
       Standing in the need of prayer.
   (ii) There is none other Man fighteth for us, but only
        Thou, O Lord.
   (iii) Belial, than *whom* a spirit more lewd fell not from
         heaven.
   (iv) *Whom* say men that I am ?
   (v) Excuse *my* going first.

CHAPTER X

ANALYSIS OF THE SIMPLE SENTENCE

I. Subject and Predicate

It has been noted earlier in this book (pp. 12-13) that every simple sentence can be divided into two parts:

1. The Subject—the part which names what we are thinking about.

2. The Predicate—the part which makes a statement about the subject.

Examples:

(i) *Viola loved Orsino.*

Subject	Predicate
Viola	loved Orsino.

(ii) *Viola was Sebastian's twin sister.*

Subject	Predicate
Viola	was Sebastian's twin sister.

(iii) *Maria, Sir Toby Belch, Sir Andrew and Fabian hatched a plot against Malvolio.*

Subject	Predicate
Maria, Sir Toby Belch, Sir Andrew and Fabian	hatched a plot against Malvolio.

Consider the first sentence again: *Viola loved Orsino.*

Subject: Viola
Predicate: loved Orsino.

The predicate here contains two ideas:

(i) The action *loved.*
(ii) The sufferer of the action *Orsino.*

The action of the verb passes over to an object. We can show the passing over with a vertical line down in the following manner :

Subject		*Predicate*
Viola———————		————loved
		Orsino (Object)

Let the sentence read now as follows :

> *Fair Viola loved Orsino dearly*.

The sentence would be divided into subject and predicate as follows :

Subject	*Predicate*
Fair Viola	loved Orsino dearly

The noun in the subject *Viola* is qualified by the adjective *fair*. The verb in the predicate is qualified by the adverb *dearly*. The sentence could be analysed thus :

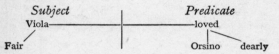

The division of the sentence in this way is called Graphic Analysis ; by it we can show easily how the component parts of the sentence are linked together. The line connecting an adjective with the noun it qualifies is written ╱ : e.g.

noun

╱

adjective

The line connecting an adverb with a verb which it qualifies is written ╲ : e.g.

verb

╲

adverb

This graphic method is one way of showing the analysis of a sentence. There are other methods, but perhaps this is the simplest.

II. Steps in Analysis

The analysis of a sentence might be undertaken in the steps shown in the following example :

> The foolish Malvolio reprimanded the drunken knight severely.

Step 1. Find the verb. *Reprimanded.*

Step 2. Find the subject-word. The subject can be found by putting *who ?* or *what ?* before the verb. Who reprimanded ? *Malvolio.*

Step 3. We can now divide the sentence mentally into subject and predicate. We also know the subject-word and the verb in the predicate.

Subject	*Predicate*
the foolish *Malvolio*———	———*reprimanded* the drunken knight severely

Step 4. Are there any words qualifying the subject-word ? *The foolish.*

(*Note :* The, a, an, are really adjectives since they go with the nouns. They have lost their adjectival force. *The* is known as the definite article. *A, an,* are known as the indefinite articles.)

Subject	*Predicate*
Malvolio———	———reprimanded the drunken knight severely
the foolish	

Step 5. Is there any object ? The object can be found by putting *whom ?* or *what ?* after the verb. Reprimanded whom ? *The drunken knight.* Object : *The drunken knight.*

Step 6. Is there any word qualifying the object ? *The drunken.*

Subject	*Predicate*
Malvolio———	———reprimanded
the foolish	knight
	the drunken

Step 7. What remains in the sentence ? *Severely.* *Severely* states how the foolish Malvolio reprimanded the drunken knight. It is an *Adverb of Manner.*

D *

Final analysis :

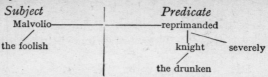

Subject
Malvolio
the foolish

Predicate
reprimanded
knight   severely
the drunken

Exercise 126.—Analyse the following sentences graphically :

1. Olivia mourns. 2. Viola attended the court. 3. Sir Andrew talked foolishly. 4. Sir Toby was dancing a caper. 5. The witty clown sang a merry song. 6. The rain raineth every day. 7. Sir Andrew and Viola fought a duel. 8. Viola visited the countess regularly. 9. The four plotters watched Malvolio eagerly. 10. They laid him in a darkened room.

III. The Indirect Object

It has been seen that a verb may sometimes take two objects :

> e.g. Sebastian gave Sir Andrew a heavy blow.

The sentence contains two objects :

(i) the thing given : *a blow.*
(ii) the person to whom the thing is given : *Sir Andrew*

The " thing given " is called the Direct Object, as the action of the transitive verb *directly* passes over to it.

The second object is called the Indirect Object, because it denotes a person or thing *for whom* or *to whom* an action is done.

The indirect object is represented in graphic analysis as follows :

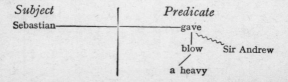

Subject
Sebastian

Predicate
gave
blow   Sir Andrew
a heavy

Exercise 127.—Analyse the following sentences graphically :

1. The clown afforded the court much amusement. 2. Viola gave him some money. 3. Malvolio showed Olivia the letter. 4. She refused him his offer. 5. Sir Andrew fondly offered her his hand. 6. Pert little Maria told the others her well-kept secret.

IV. The Complement

Examine the sentences :

> (i) William saw the captain.
> (ii) William was the captain.

In sentence (i) the word *captain* is the direct object of the verb *saw*. The words *William* and *captain* stand for different persons.

In sentence (ii) the nouns *captain* and *William* refer to the same person. Sentence (ii) is built up as follows :

1. Subject.
2. Verb.
3. A noun in the predicate, referring to the subject. This is called a Predicative Noun referring to the subject. It helps to complete the sense of the predicate.

William was by itself does not make sense. In analysis, a predicative word is often called the Complement, because it completes the sense of the verb. In a similar way, an adjective may complete the sense of a verb to form the predicate :

> e.g. William was clever.
> The roses were white.

Clever, white are predicative adjectives or complements.

Exercise 128.—Supply suitable predicative nouns to complete the sense of the following :

1. John is —. 2. Chaucer was —. 3. Mary will be —. 4. The lieutenant can be —. 5. The baron was made —.

Exercise 129.—Supply suitable predicative adjectives to complete the sense of the following :

1. The night is —.   2. The wind was —.   3. The sea will be —.   4. The path is becoming —.   5. Your duty is —.

Consider the use of the verb *turns* in the following sentences:

        (i) The wheel turns slowly.
       (ii) The captain turns the wheel.
      (iii) The knight turns pale.

In sentence (i) *slowly* tells how the wheel turns.

    Slowly is an adverb of manner.

In sentence (ii) *the wheel* tells what the captain turns, and is the object of the verb *turns*.

In sentence (iii) *pale* is an adjective describing *knight* and is a predicative adjective referring to the subject.   The verb *turns* is here the equivalent of *is* or *becomes*.

Exercise 130.—State whether the words italicised in the following are (1) the objects of the verb, or (2) adverbs, or (3) complements :

1. The king grows *kind*.   2. The farmers grow *barley* on this field.   3. The baby grows very *quickly*.   4. The siren sounded the *alarm*.   5. It sounds *simple*.   6. I feel *better today*.   7. I can feel his *heart*.   8. It was so cold that we could scarcely feel *properly*.   9. Don't get *angry*. 10. Get your *coat*.   11. Get *along*.   12. *Suddenly* she stopped. 13. I stopped that *noise*.   14. She stopped *still*.   15. She seems *nervous*.   16. He is not what he *always* seems.

V. Graphic Analysis of Complement

For the purpose of Graphic Analysis the predicative words are shown as a continuation of the verb, because they are completing or continuing its sense :

e.g. Sentence (i) *William was King*.

Subject	Predicate
William———————	———was——King

Sentence (ii) *Nelson was our greatest Admiral.*

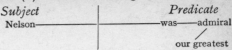

Subject	Predicate
Nelson——————	———was——admiral
	our greatest

Exercise 131.—Analyse the following sentences graphically :

1. Britain is an island.   2. Her fields are green.   3. The barons became powerful.   4. This unprovoked abuse appeared unjust.   5. The merry laughter seemed inappropriate.   6. His latest play is considered his masterpiece. 7. The milk has turned sour.   8. His ambition is universal control.   9. His steps became slower and shorter.   10. He is tall and dark and handsome.

VI. Further Graphic Analysis

Thus far we have considered the analysis of the sentence which takes the form of a statement. It will be remembered that there are four kinds of simple sentences :

(i) A statement.   (iii) A command.
(ii) A question.   (iv) An exclamation.

The Question Sentence.

(*a*) Consider the following pairs of sentences :

(i) Who invented Wireless Telegraphy ?
(ii) Marconi invented Wireless Telegraphy.

In these two sentences the verb is the same : *invented.*
The object is the same : *Wireless Telegraphy.*

The difference between the sentences is that in sentence (ii) we are told *who* invented Wireless. *Marconi* is, therefore, the subject. In sentence (i) *who*, introducing the question, has to stand for that unknown person. *Who* is the subject of the verb *invented.*

Graphic analysis :

Subject	Predicate
Who——————	———invented
	Wireless Telegraphy ?

The word *Who* is an *Interrogative Pronoun.*

(*b*) The word introducing the question is not always the subject. It may be the object.

Sentence (iii) What are you reading ?
        (iv) You are reading " Punch."

What and *Punch* are the object of *are reading*.

Query : What part of speech is *what* ?

(*c*) Sentence (v) What is your name ?
        (vi) Your name is MacTavish.

What and *MacTavish* complete the sense of the verb *is* and are predicative words.

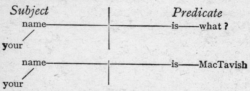

Queries : What kind of predicative word is *MacTavish* ?
          What kind of predicative word is *what* ?

(*d*) Sentence (vii) When are the troops leaving ?
         (viii) The troops are leaving tomorrow.

The adverb of time *tomorrow* answers the question introduced by *when* ?

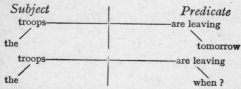

(*e*) Some question-sentences are merely a rearrangement of the order of words in a statement-sentence.

Sentence (ix) *Can you drive a car?* is an inversion of *You can drive a car.*

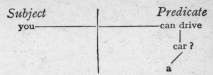

Subject	Predicate
you————	—can drive
	car?
	a

Exercise 132.—Analyse the following sentences graphically :

1. Who killed Cock Robin?   2. Who goes there?
3. What are you doing?   4. Whom do you want?
5. How did they manage?   6. Where is the unfortunate child going?   7. Why did she leave me?   8. Does he recognise me yet?   9. Why did the wily king refuse him admittance?   10. What will the old farmer probably offer him tomorrow?

The Command Sentence.

Consider the following sentences :

> (i) Go carefully.
> (ii) Slope arms !

The verbs *go, slope* are addressed to a person or persons listening to the instruction. The real significance of the command is therefore :

> (i) (You) go carefully.   (ii) (You) slope arms !

The subject is not definitely stated but implied. It is said to be an *understood* subject. The graphic analysis is as follows :

Subject	Predicate
(you)————	—go
	carefully
(you)————	—slope
	arms !

> (iii) Jones, come here.

In this sentence, where the person who is being commanded is addressed by name, the subject is still the understood subject (You). The word *Jones* plays no part in the structure of the sentence and is not included in the analysis :

Person addressed : *Jones*, Vocative Case.

Exercise 133.—Analyse the following command-sentences graphically :

1. Halt ! 2. Look yonder ! 3. Mind your heads ! 4. Be quiet ! 5. Give me your hand ! 6. Appear unmoved. 7. My son, give me your heart. 8. Don't do that ! 9. Ask me another. 10. Friends, Romans, Countrymen, lend me your ears.

The Exclamation Sentence.

Examine :

    (i) How the wind howled !
    (ii) What courage she has !
    (iii) What a bully you are !

Sentence (i) is an exclamation, introduced by *how* indicating manner.

The graphic analysis is, therefore :

In sentence (ii) the exclamation is introduced by *what*.

The analysis is :

Sentence (iii) What a bully you are !

In this sentence the exclamation is expressed in the complement :

Subject | Predicate
you————————————are———what a bully !

Consider another sentence :

Sentence (iv) Oh ! we have lost the train.

This sentence is a statement, not an exclamation. It is introduced by an exclamation of disappointment, but the word " Oh " plays no part in the structure of the sentence.

Exercise 134.—Analyse the following exclamation-sentences :

1. How the fire burns ! 2. What a noise you are making ! 3. What the visitors must have thought ! 4. What an evil influence he always exerts ! 5. What a mean woman she is ! 6. How merrily ring the bells !

Exercise 135.—(i) State whether the following sentences are statements, questions, commands or exclamations. (ii) Analyse the sentences.

1. How were they behaving ? 2. How they were behaving ! 3. What has the old king done ? 4. What the old king has done ! 5. My word ! The old king has done a noble work. 6. What an attractive manner she has ! 7. Has she an attractive manner ? 8. Gracious ! She has an unattractive manner. 9. Improve your manners, young man. 10. How joyfully they gave their foes their deserts ! 11. I must ask you your name. 12. The oldest inhabitant told me an interesting yarn yesterday.

Revision

1. Divide the following sentences into subject and predicate :

   (i) The heathen in his blindness bows down to wood and stone.

   (ii) The merry brown hares came leaping over the crest of the hill.

   (iii) My fairest child, I have no song to give you.

   (iv) No lark could pipe to skies so dull and grey.

   (v) What, then, does Dr. Newman mean ?

   (vi) All the world's a stage.

2. Analyse the following sentences graphically.

  (i) Sweet are the uses of *adversity*.

 (ii) This our life, exempt from public haunt,
      Finds tongues in trees, books in the running brooks,
      Sermons in stones, and good in everything.

 (iii) Come *you* from old Bellario ?

 (iv) Fear no more the *heat* of the sun.

  (v) Then must the Jew be merciful.

 (vi) Is Horatio here ?

 (vii) What a *piece* of work is man !

(viii) The very substance of the ambitious is merely the *shadow* of a dream.

 (ix) Friends, Romans, countrymen, lend *me* your ears.

  (x) Heat *me* these irons hot.

3. Write a note on the case of the words in italics.

CHAPTER XI

EQUIVALENTS

I. Adjectival Equivalents

We have seen that the simple sentences can be analysed graphically as follows:

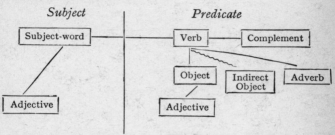

It does not, of course, mean that every sentence conforms to this model and has each one of these parts. For instance, if the verb is intransitively used, there is no object.

1. *Adjectival Equivalents.*—It has been noted earlier in this book that it is sometimes found more convenient to use an adjectival phrase or clause when describing a noun.

(*a*) *In the Subject.*

Consider the following sentences:

(1) The early settlers had treated the natives shamefully.

The idea contained in the word *early* might be expanded into an adjectival phrase:

(2) The settlers *arriving first on the island* had treated the natives shamefully.

Or into a sentence:

(3) The settlers, *who arrived first on the island,* had treated the natives shamefully.

The adjectival equivalent in sentence 3 contains both subject (*who*) and predicate (*arrived first on the island*). It is thus a sentence enclosed in a larger sentence and it is called a Clause, from the Latin *clausus*, meaning *closed*. A clause which is used as an equivalent of an adjective is called an *Adjectival Clause*. A clause used instead of a noun is called a *Noun Clause*. A clause used instead of an adverb is called an *Adverbial Clause*.

Such sentences could be analysed graphically thus:

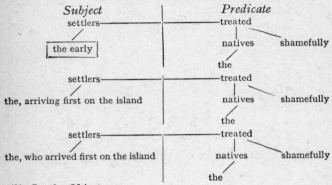

(b) *In the Object*:

Sentence (4) We met a reputed statesman.

(5) We met a statesman of great reputation.

(6) We met a statesman who had an international reputation.

In sentence (4) the object is qualified by an adjective, in sentence (5) by an adjectival phrase, in sentence (6) by an adjectival clause.

Analysis:

        Subject   *Predicate*

(4)   we————————————met

                             statesman

                         a reputed

(5)   we————————————met

                             statesman

                    a, of great reputation

(6)

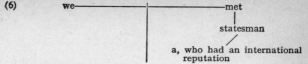

(c) In the Complement :

Sentence (7) It was a skilful game.
        (8) It was a game of skill.
        (9) It was a game which demanded consider-
            able skill.

In sentence (7) the noun in the complement is qualified by an adjective, in sentence (8) by an adjectival phrase, in sentence (9) by an adjectival clause.

Analysis :

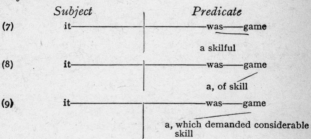

(d) There is another form of enlargement to the subject.

Consider the following sentence :

    The burglar, *who had already served a sentence in prison,* was tried at the County Court.

The words *in italics* are an adjectival clause qualifying *burglar.*

Another form of the sentence might be :

    The burglar, *an ex-convict,* was tried at the County Court.

The words *an ex-convict* refer to the same person as the word *burglar.* As they are used together, *an ex-convict* is said to be in apposition to the noun *burglar.* It is another form of the adjective equivalent.

Analysis :

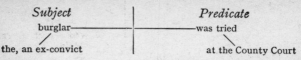

Subject	Predicate
burglar————	————was tried
the, an ex-convict	at the County Court

In a similar way, the nouns in apposition are used in the object :

e.g. The Governors appointed Mr. Robson, an old Etonian.

Subject	Predicate
Governors————	————appointed
the	Mr. Robson
	an old Etonian

Exercise 136.—Substitute nouns in apposition for adjectival clauses in the following sentences :

1. My friend, *who had served many years in the Navy*, predicted the approach of a storm. 2. Mr. Simpkins, *who will be elected Mayor next year*, has a large business in the town. 3. I am reading a book by Scott, *who is my favourite author*. 4. We are renting a house *which overlooks the Broads*. 5. The blacksmith, *who had the strength of a Hercules*, won the weight-lifting competition.

Exercise 137.—Analyse the following sentences graphically:

1. Woolworth's have bought the shop at the corner. 2. The clown with the blue nose was very popular. 3. The building, which stands high on a hill, has a commanding position. 4. We suddenly realised the danger which confronted us. 5. Mr. Roberts, a man of many years' mining experience, detected the fatal smell. 6. My brother Bob owes your brother Bob a bob. 7. Are you addressing me, your protector and friend, thus ? 8. The sentry, overcome with fatigue, slept at his post. 9. The soldiers, shouting wildly, scaled the walls surrounding the castle. 10. The stream which winds slowly through pleasant meadows eventually becomes a broad river. 11. Bring me my bow of burning gold. 12. What an experience of life his travel will bring him !

II. Adverbial Equivalents

Similarly, the verb may be qualified in the predicate by an adverb, or adverbial equivalent, in the form of a phrase or a clause.

(*a*) *Manner*.

Consider the following sentences :

(1) The master repaid his servants *fairly*.
(2) The master repaid his servants *with all fairness*.
(3) The master repaid his servants *as they deserved*.

Fairly is an adverb of manner. *With all fairness* is a phrase doing the work of an adverb of manner. In the graphic analysis of the sentence, the adverbial phrase or adverbial clause may be joined to the verb it qualifies in the same manner as an adverb. The adverb, the phrase and the clause answer the question *How ?*

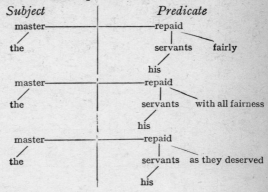

(*b*) *Time*.

Consider the following sentences :

(4) I arose *early*.
(5) I arose *at dawn of day*.
(6) I arose *as soon as it was light*.

The adverb *early*, the adverbial phrase, *at dawn of day*, the adverbial clause, *as soon as it was light*, qualify the verb *arose* by answering the question *When ?* They indicate *time*.

Analysis :

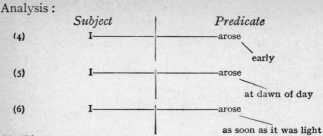

	Subject		*Predicate*
(4)	I		arose
			early
(5)	I		arose
			at dawn of day
(6)	I		arose
			as soon as it was light

(c) *Place*.

Consider the following sentences :

    (7) The aeroplane crashed *here*.
    (8) The aeroplane crashed *on this spot*.
    (9) The aeroplane crashed *where it did no damage*.

The adverb *here*, the adverbial phrase, *on this spot*, the adverbial clause, *where it did no damage*, qualify the verb *crashed*, by answering the question *Where?* They are adverbs or adverbial equivalents of *place*.

Analysis :

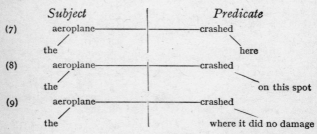

	Subject		*Predicate*
(7)	aeroplane		crashed
	the		here
(8)	aeroplane		crashed
	the		on this spot
(9)	aeroplane		crashed
	the		where it did no damage

Exercise 138.—Give three adverbial equivalents for each of the following adverbs of interrogation (e.g. When ? *When* shall I expect you ? *At what time* shall I expect you ?) : Where ? How ? Why ?

Exercise 139.—Analyse the following sentences :

    1. The fishing smacks sailed away.   2. They left the harbour at dusk.   3. The Atlantic rollers beat against the

vessels.   4. On most occasions they had a good catch.
5. By midnight, the wind was blowing with terrific force.
6. When dawn came, the wind dropped.   7. They were
leaving the storm in their rear.   8. By what means did
the men catch their fish ?   9. After three days at sea they
returned to harbour.   10. The fishermen were rewarded
as they deserved with a large catch.   11. Wherever they
sailed, they always faced danger.   12. With what fascina-
tion are these men drawn to the sea !

Exercise 140.—Construct sentences using the following
expressions as (i) adjectival equivalents ; (ii) adverbial
equivalents (e.g. at the top of the hill : The house *at the top
of the hill* is vacant (adjectival).   We rested *at the top of
the hill* (adverbial)) :

(1) round the corner ;   (2) in the streets ;   (3) with a
rake ;   (4) across the meadows ;   (5) in the tree-tops ;   (6) on
the high seas.

III. Noun Equivalents

Consider the following sentences:

(1) We knew the route.
(2) We knew where to go.
(3) We knew that the road led to Penrith.

In sentence (1) the object of the verb *knew* is the noun
route.   In sentence (2) the object of the verb *knew* is the
phrase, *where to go*.   In sentence (3) the object of the verb
knew is a clause, *that the road led to Penrith*.
Where to go is a phrase acting as a noun equivalent.
That the road led to Penrith is a clause acting as a noun
equivalent.

Exercise 141.—(*a*) Substitute suitable nouns for the
italicised phrases used as noun equivalents in the following :

1. The professional showed us *how to play*.   2. Will you
tell me *when to stand* ?   3. *To swim before breakfast* is most
exhilarating.   4. Tell me *where to go for a doctor*.   5. Advise
me *what to say*.

(b) Substitute suitable nouns for the italicised clauses as noun equivalents in the following :

1. The Prime Minister announced *when the house would adjourn*. 2. Can you tell me *what the time is*? 3. The farmer knew *where he could best graze his cattle*. 4. The owner told us *that the house was most attractive*. 5. We discovered *where the ammunition was hidden*.

(c) Replace the nouns in italics by equivalent noun clauses :

1. I want to see the newspaper *account*. 2. The judge solemnly announced the *verdict*. 3. Tell me your *opinion*. 4. The reason is a *mystery*. 5. We visited Goethe's *birthplace*.

Exercise 142.—Analyse the following sentences graphically :

1. Uncle Remus often visits us. 2. He never knows when to leave. 3. He has a great weakness for talking. 4. How to keep him quiet is a real problem. 5. Uncle Remus does not appreciate that silence is golden. 6. We often do not know how to avoid being angry. 7. Ask him what he did in the Great War. 8. Twinkling his eye, he will begin forthwith. 9. I cannot discover why he talks so much. 10. He is a man of considerable powers of conversation.

Revision

1. Explain the meaning of the following expressions :

   (i) Adjectival equivalent, adverbial equivalent, noun equivalent.
   (ii) Predicative adjective, adverb of degree, nominative absolute.
   (iii) Transitive, intransitive.
   (iv) Active voice, passive voice.
   (v) The complement.

2. Read the following passage and answer the questions underneath :

> I am an intellectual chap
> And think of things that would astonish you.
> I often think it's comical
> How nature always does contrive
> That every boy and every girl,
> That's born into the world alive,
> Is either a little Liberal
> Or else a little Conservative.

Pick out the following :

   (i) Two adjectives of quality.

  (ii) A distributive adjective.

 (iii) Two adjectival equivalents.

 (iv) An adverb.

  (v) Adverbial (phrase) equivalent.

CHAPTER XII

KINDS OF SENTENCES

We have noticed three kinds of word-groups: the Phrase, the Clause, the Sentence.

I. Phrases

A phrase is a group of words making incomplete sense.

(i) A phrase may be introduced by a preposition:

e.g. *under* the earth; *beyond* his strength; *for* three weeks.

These could be called *prepositional* phrases.

(ii) A phrase may be introduced by an infinitive:

e.g. *to find* the answer; *to open* the door; *to bury* the hatchet.

These could be called *infinitive* phrases.

(iii) A phrase may be introduced by a participle:

e.g. *having lived* a carefree life; *being* an honest man; *leading* the team on to the field.

These could be called *participial* phrases.

Exercise 143.—(*a*) Use the following prepositional phrases in sentences (e.g. in time: The cheque arrived just *in time* to meet his bills):

in former times; to time; at times; with time to spare; out of time; for seven times.

(*b*) Suggest similar prepositional phrases with the word *hand*.

Exercise 144.—Construct sentences which illustrate the use of the following:

(i) Prepositional phrases (e.g. He came by *in a hurry*): in a fix; out of sorts; under a cloud; beyond the pale; on board.

(ii) Infinitive phrases (e.g. I want *to bury* the hatchet) :

to turn over a new leaf ; to put the cart before the horse ; to carry coals to Newcastle ; to rob Peter to pay Paul ; to hit the nail on the head.

(iii) Participial Phrases (e.g. *Owning a large farm*, he felt confident to speak on the subject of agriculture) :

singing a well-known song ; holding their breath ; smiling an evil smile ; feeling their way ; coming to attention.

II. Clauses

It has been noted that a clause is a sentence-group of words enclosed in a longer sentence. The clause, like a sentence, must have a subject and predicate of its own :

e.g. *When the wind blows*, the cradle will rock.

It will be necessary at a later stage to deal more fully with the various types of clauses that are found in sentences.

Exercise 145.—Complete the proverbs from which the following clauses are taken :

when the cat is away ; before they are hatched ; while the sun shines ; if the cap fits ; that glitters ; that has no turning ; who laughs last ; where there is smoke ; silence is golden ; sow a thought.

Exercise 146.—Construct sentences using the following clauses (i) as noun clauses, (ii) as adverbial clauses, (iii) as adjectival clauses (e.g. When the tide turns : (i) Do you know *when the tide turns*? (Noun). (ii) *When the tide turns* we will put out to sea (Adverbial). (iii) The time *when the tide turns* varies each day (Adjectival)) :

(1) when the work is finished ; (2) when my ship comes home ; (3) where the doctor lives.

Mr. Jingle plays Cricket

In Charles Dickens' book, " Pickwick Papers," there is a character named Alfred Jingle, who speaks in a jerky breathless style, preferring phrases and broken sentences to complete sentences, as if he were a human telegram. Here is his unusual account of an equally unusual cricket match :

Played a match once—single wicket—friend the Colonel —Sir Thomas Blazo—who should get the greatest number of runs—won the toss—first innings—seven o'clock a.m.— six natives to look out—went in, kept in, heat intense— natives all fainted—taken away—fresh half-dozen ordered fainted also—Blazo bowling—supported by two natives— couldn't bowl out—fainted too, cleared away the colonel— wouldn't give in—faithful attendant—Quanko Samba—last man left—sun so hot—bat in blisters—ball scorched brown —five hundred and seventy runs—rather exhausted— Quanko mustered up last remaining strength—bowled me out—had a bath and went to dinner.

Exercise 147.—Rewrite this account in consecutive and straightforward sentences.

III. Sentences

The third word-group is the **Sentence,** which is a group of words making complete sense and expressing a complete thought. Considered from the point of view of structure, sentences are classified as follows :

(i) Simple. (ii) Double. (iii) Multiple. (iv) Complex.

Consider the sentences that make up the following passage :

(a) 1. Charles Lamb met Coleridge in the Strand. 2. Coleridge held Lamb by the top button of his coat and Lamb was obliged to listen to a flood of eloquence from his friend. 3. Coleridge would not stop talking and Lamb feared missing his appointment but he did not wish to offend his friend. 4. Whilst Coleridge held on tightly to the button, Lamb snipped it off with a pair of pocket scissors.

(b) 5. Lamb then went on his way. 6. He completed his errand and then returned the same way. 7. He entered the Strand and there was Coleridge and he was still talking. 8. Coleridge, who was busily engaged talking to the button, had not missed his friend.

There are four sentences in section (a) of the above passage. Count the number of verbs in each sentence. Let us begin with the first sentence.

(i) The Simple Sentence

There is one verb in the first sentence : *met*. A sentence containing *one* finite verb, either expressed or understood, is said to be a *Simple* sentence. The word *Simple* sentence does not refer to the content of the sentence ; nor does it refer to the length. It means that it has *one* finite verb.

1. *Longer Simple Sentences.*

Consider the sentence : Charles Lamb, walking down the Strand on his way from the City to Westminster, met Samuel Taylor Coleridge, the poet, philosopher and critic, coming in the opposite direction.

This is a long sentence, but from the grammatical point of view it is a *simple* sentence, BECAUSE IT HAS ONE FINITE VERB.

Query 1 : What is the finite verb ?

Query 2 : Find the simple sentence in part (*b*) of the passage.

2. *The Double Subject.*

Consider the sentence : Charles Lamb and his sister wrote the " Tales from Shakespeare."

There is a double subject in this sentence—*Charles Lamb* and *his sister*. But there is only one finite verb, *wrote*. The sentence is therefore a simple sentence with a double subject. The conjunction *and* is joining words, not clauses. Similarly, you may find in a simple sentence a double object (e.g. Lamb wrote *essays* and *poetry*), or a pair of adjectives qualifying a noun or a pair of adverbs qualifying a verb. But if there is one finite verb, it is a simple sentence.

3. *Elliptical Sentence.*

If you were asked, " What is your name ? " you might reply, " John Smith." If the question was, " What is the time ? " the reply might be, " Six o'clock." It is unlikely that we should answer with a full sentence, " My name is John Smith," or, " The time is six o'clock." Our shorter replies, " John Smith," " Six o'clock," mean the same thing.

According to the rule that has been most carefully empha-sised, a sentence must contain a finite verb. Can our replies, " John Smith," " Six o'clock," be regarded as sentences? In their normal context, *John Smith* and *six o'clock* are words, not sentences, but in their present context they serve to make the complete sense of the sentence, the finite verb being readily understood. Such sentences are called Elliptical (from Greek—" to leave out ").

John Smith is an elliptical sentence, the equivalent of *My name is John Smith*. *Six o'clock* is an elliptical sen-tence, the equivalent of *The time is six o'clock*.

Exercise 148.—Write out the following elliptical sentences as full sentences containing a finite verb :

1. No smoking in the lift. 2. Passengers off the car first. 3. Plenty of room on top. 4. Hands up ! 5. The more, the merrier. 6. Tickets, please ! 7. Price of petrol up again. 8. What about it ? 9. Slow ! 10. You coward !

(ii) The Double Sentence

Now look at sentence 2 in the passage, i.e. *Coleridge held Lamb by the top button of his coat and Lamb was obliged to listen to a flood of eloquence from his friend*.

There are two finite verbs in this sentence : *held*, *was obliged*. The sentence is made up of two clauses, each con-taining a finite verb and joined by the conjunction *and*. Neither of the two clauses in the sentence is dependent on the other for its grammatical function. Such clauses are said to be co-ordinate (of the same rank) and the con-junction that joins them is a co-ordinating conjunction. Such a sentence is called a *Double Sentence*, a name which explains itself. There are really two sentences joined by a conjunction. Sometimes such sentences are called Com-pound Sentences. If the subject of the second clause is the same as the subject of the first, it is often omitted in the second :

e.g. Wesley preached in every part of England and (he) attracted crowds everywhere.

Query : Find a double sentence in section (b) of the passage.

It should be noted that either of the clauses in a double sentence could include an adjectival or adverbial or noun clause.

E.g. *As soon as he saw him, Coleridge held Lamb by the top button of his coat, and Lamb was obliged to listen to a flood of eloquence from his friend.*

The sentence would be analysed thus :

Coleridge held Lamb by the top button of his coat		(Co-ordinate Clause.)
he saw him	Link—as soon as	(Adverbial Clause.)
Lamb was obliged to listen . . . his friend	Link—and	(Co-ordinate Clause.)

Similarly, there may be a noun or an adjectival clause in either or both of the co-ordinate clauses. This point will be treated in detail later.

(iii) The Multiple Sentence

Notice sentence 3 in the passage. It is made up of three clauses :

1. Coleridge would not stop talking.
2. Lamb feared missing his appointment.
3. He did not wish to offend his friend.

This sentence represents a further development of the double sentence, where there were two co-ordinate clauses. In this sentence there are three co-ordinate clauses, the first two joined by the co-ordinating conjunction *and*, and the last two by the co-ordinating conjunction *but*. A sentence containing three or more co-ordinate clauses, each of which may have dependent adjectival, adverbial or noun clauses, is called a Multiple Sentence.

Query : Find a multiple sentence in section (*b*) of the passage.

Exercise 149.—Use the following groups of sentences as co-ordinate clauses to form double or multiple sentences :

1. An explorer met a lion. No more was heard of the explorer. 2. I knocked twice. I received no answer. 3. Stone walls do not a prison make. Iron bars do not make a cage. 4. The occupant informed the police. The

E

police telephoned to the Fire Service.　5. Men may come. Men may go.　I go on for ever.　6. His car is very old.　It makes a deafening noise.　It is most reliable.　7. No man can serve two masters.　He will hate the one.　He will serve the other.　He will serve the one.　He will hate the other.

Exercise 150.—State whether the following sentences are simple, double or multiple :

1. The Eiffel Tower is a famous landmark and can be seen for miles around.　2. The tide of battle now flowed against them but their courage was undiminished.　3. The searchers looked for the lost child on the desolate mountain ridges, in the hidden grass, over the wide and rolling woodland and in the dense woods.　4. Hearing a cry of fear coming from a disused sheepfold, one of the searchers ran to the spot to find a child lying exhausted, with terror-stricken eyes. 5. The search was over, the lost child was found.　6. I came, I saw, I conquered.　7. The pair had walked in silence for nearly an hour when one of them broke the silence.　8. The sailor had brought back with him sundry treasures from the East, including a parrot, a monkey, some trinkets to adorn his mother's home and some gold to fill the innkeeper's pocket.　9. The way was long, the wind was cold, the minstrel was infirm and old.　10. Just for a handful of silver he left us ; just for a ribbon to stick in his coat.

Exercise 151.—Rewrite the following double sentences as simple sentences (e.g. Double : *I offered him my help but he refused it*.　Simple : *He refused my offered help*) :

1. There was a thunderstorm and the picnic was spoilt. 2. The heat was terrific and no serious tennis could be played.　3. The hunt was still in progress and then darkness fell.　4. He tried all manner of schemes but they all failed.　5. I was astonished and could not speak.　6. She was a beautiful girl and was admired by many.　7. Peggy was taken ill and the holiday had to be postponed.　8. He was dressed most unconventionally.　The villagers laughed at him.　9. The roar of the aeroplanes was deafening.　We could not hear ourselves speak.　10. We were three goals down at half-time, but we eventually won the match and everyone was surprised.

(iv) The Complex Sentence

Consider sentence 4 in the Lamb extract : *Whilst Coleridge held on tightly to the button, Lamb snipped it off with a pair of pocket scissors.*

There are two clauses in this sentence :

1. Lamb snipped it off with a pair of pocket scissors.
2. Whilst Coleridge held on tightly to the button.

Clause 2 depends for its significance upon clause 1—it states the time of the action. Clause 2 is therefore of lower rank or *subordinate* to clause 1. Clause 1 is therefore called the Main or Principal Clause. Clause 2 is called the Subordinate Clause or the Dependent Clause.

A sentence made up of a main clause and one or more subordinate clauses is called a Complex Sentence.

The subordinate clause may be one of the following :

> (*a*) An Adjectival Clause.
> (*b*) An Adverbial Clause.
> (*c*) A Noun Clause.

Reference has been made earlier to these types of clauses, but it is necessary now to examine them in closer detail.

A. ADJECTIVAL CLAUSES.

We have already discussed adjectival clauses, and something of what follows may serve as a revision.

1. Consider the sentence : People who live in glass-houses should not throw stones.

There are two finite verbs in this sentence : (i) live, (ii) should throw. There are thus two clauses :

> (i) People should not throw stones.
> (ii) Who live in glass-houses.

The clause, *who live in glass-houses*, adds to the meaning of *people*. It is an adjectival clause qualifying the noun *people*. It is a clause subordinate to the main clause : *people should not throw stones.*

Subject	Predicate
people———————	———should throw
who live in glass-houses	stones not

Adjectival clauses may be joined to their main clauses by :
  (i) Relative pronouns : who, whom, which, that, what, as, etc.
  (ii) Relative adjectives : whose.
  (iii) Relative adverbs : where, when, why.

Exercise 152.—Name the main clauses and subordinate adjectival clauses in the following sentences :

1. There was once a man who fell asleep during a sermon. 2. He had a dream which was most terrifying in character. 3. He was being led to the gallows by a masked man who was going to hang him.   4. The hangman, whom he asked to spare him, proceeded with his duty.   5. At this point the man's wife, who was ashamed to see her husband asleep in church, tapped him on the neck.   6. The good woman, whose intention was to awaken her husband, had done the worst possible thing.   7. Her husband, who in his dream was awaiting execution, died of shock.   8. A friend of mine who heard this story saw in it a flaw, which you ought also to see.

2. *Omission of the Relative Pronoun.*—When the relative pronoun is in the object case, it is often omitted :   e.g. *Take back the ring you gave me*, for *Take back the ring that you gave me.*   If the relative pronoun is omitted, it must be *understood* in the analysis of the sentence.
Main Clause : Take back the ring.
Subordinate Adjectival Clause : (that) you gave me.

Exercise 153.—Name the main and subordinate adjectival clauses in the following sentences :

1. Give to me the life I love.   2. He repeated the news he had just heard.   3. The story you told was not appreciated in that company.   4. Gibraltar was the next port we called at.   5. The book I am reading deals with the French Revolution.   6. The good he does outweighs the evil influence his brother exerts.

3. *The Co-ordinating Use of the Relative.*—Consider the following sentences :

Comparatively few aircraft can operate at thirty-five thousand feet, which simplifies the task of identification.

There are two clauses :

(i) Comparatively few aircraft can operate at thirty-five thousand feet.

(ii) Which simplifies the task of identification.

The second clause wears the appearance of an adjectival clause. It looks as if it is introduced by a relative pronoun. But look again. Does the clause introduced by *which* qualify any noun in the main clause ? Does it qualify " aircraft " ? " feet " ? *Which* refers back to the whole preceding clause. The real significance is :

Comparatively few aircraft can operate at thirty-five thousand feet, and *this fact* simplifies, etc. . . .

In this sentence, then, *which simplifies the task of identification* is not an adjectival clause but another main clause, co-ordinate with the first clause. *Which* has a co-ordinating value.

Exercise 154.—In the following sentences state whether the clauses in italics are subordinate adjectival clauses or co-ordinate clauses :

1. The captain was killed in the early stages of the battle, *which was a pity*. 2. The captain, *who was an inspiring leader*, was hit by a stray bullet. 3. In the early stages of the battle *which was to last four days* the captain was killed. 4. The day *when Peace was signed* brought great rejoicing. 5. The motorist had a tyre burst at the first bend, *which was a great disappointment to him*. 6. Do you know the man *who has bought " The Laurels "* ? 7. The shadowy form proved to be only a withered tree, *which was a great relief to the girls*. 8. The centre-forward passed the ball to the captain, *who scored a perfect shot*.

4. *Correct Construction.*

(1) *Proximity.*—The adjectival clause should be found as close as possible to the word it qualifies, to avoid all possible ambiguity. " Punch " is constantly drawing attention to the humorous interpretations suggested in sentences where this rule is overlooked.

Consider the following :

Some tinfoil was placed in the sun which was thinly covered with a layer of wax.

It is obvious that the adjectival clause, *which was thinly covered with a layer of wax*, should qualify the noun *tinfoil*. The adjectival clause should therefore be placed nearer to its antecedent to avoid the somewhat ridiculous interpretation that could otherwise be given :

e.g. Some tinfoil which was thinly covered with a layer of wax was placed in the sun.

Exercise 155—Rewrite the following sentences in a correct form :

1. He was given some medicine by the doctor that was distinctly unpleasant to the mouth.   2. They listened to a sermon by an old parson that was long, disjointed, but with some good points.   3. At Moreton the coach made a stop for petrol which lasted for about ten minutes.   4. There was a suite of furniture for sale, the property of an old man, that was well-upholstered and well-sprung.   5. The Management may refuse permission to anyone that it considers proper.   6. An umbrella has been lost by a gentleman that has a bone handle and steel ribs.

(2) *And who, and which.*

Consider the following sentences :

1. The fireman who saw the blaze and who rescued the trapped family received the George Cross.
2. Bruce was a man of quiet courage and purposeful determination and who had considerable qualities of leadership.

In sentence 1 there are three clauses, one main clause and two subordinate adjectival clauses qualifying the noun *fireman* :

(i) who saw the blaze.   (ii) who rescued the trapped family.

The two subordinate clauses are joined by " and." In this sentence, the relative pronoun could be omitted from the second subordinate clause :

e.g. The fireman who saw the blaze and rescued the trapped family received the George Cross.

In the next sentence there are only two finite verbs, *was* and *had*.

> Main Clause : Bruce was a man of quiet courage and
> purposeful determination.
> Subordinate Clause : who had considerable qualities of
> leadership.

It will be seen that there is one adjectival clause. *And* is then redundant or unnecessary, for there is no preceding adjectival clause as there was in sentence 1. *And who, and which* presuppose that there is a preceding clause beginning *who, which*.

The sentence could be corrected in one of the following ways :

> (i) Bruce was a man of quiet courage and purposeful
> determination, who had considerable qualities of
> leadership.

Or,

> (ii) Bruce was a man who had quiet courage and purpose-
> ful determination and who had considerable quali-
> ties of leadership.

Exercise 156.—Rewrite the following sentences in a correct form :

1. I have just read Tolstoy's " War and Peace," a book dealing with Napoleon's invasion of Russia and which is thought by many writers to be the greatest novel ever written. 2. I select books for their interest and which are full of adventure rather than information. 3. I was treated with kindness beyond all description and which I shall never forget. 4. Mr. Newlyrich bought a house of over three hundred years of age and which he immediately had equipped with all modern fittings. 5. She was a girl of infinite charm and who was loved by all her friends.

(3) *As.* The word *as* can be used as a relative pronoun introducing an adjectival clause when it follows *same, such* : e.g. She wore the same clothes *as* she wore last year.

I beheld such a spectacle *as* I shall never see again.

In these sentences *as* is used instead of *that* or *which*.

But *as* may NOT be used as an equivalent for preposition+relative :

e.g. We travelled to Winchester by the same train as the troops always travel.

In this sentence *as* denotes *by+which*. The meaning of *as* is therefore incorrectly used. It can be corrected :

(i) We travelled to Winchester by the same train by which the troops always travel.

(ii) We travelled to Winchester by the same train as the troops.

Exercise 157.—Name the adjectival clauses in the following. Correct where necessary :

1. The men made the same complaints as they had done on a previous occasion. 2. The wind was such as I have never heard before. 3. I was examined by the same doctor as I was examined for my army test. 4. I shall go to the same hotel as I did last year. 5. The patient is in about the same state as he was yesterday.

B. ADVERBIAL CLAUSES.

It has already been noted that a clause may do the work of an adverb in qualifying a verb.

1. *Adverbial Clauses of Time.*

Consider the following sentences :

(i) The men return to work *tomorrow*.

(ii) The men return to work *when the pits open*.

The word *tomorrow* answers the question *when*. It qualifies the verb *return* by telling us the time of the action. It is an adverb of Time.

In sentence 2 the clause *when the pits open* answers the question *when* and qualifies the verb *return*, telling us the time of the action. Thus *when the pits open* is an adverbial clause of Time. It is a subordinate or dependent clause qualifying *return* in the main clause, *the men return to work tomorrow*.

The subordinate clause is joined to the main clause by *when*. *When* is thus a conjunction joining two clauses.

As it introduces a subordinate clause, it is called a Sub-ordinating Conjunction. Sentence 2 can be analysed graphically :

Subject		*Predicate*
men———————		————return
the		(i) to work
		(ii) when the pits open

The men return to work : Main Clause.

the pits open : Subordinate Adverbial Clause qualifying verb *return*.

when : Link.

It should be noted that it is not necessary for the main clause to appear first in the sentence. Emphasis some-times demands a reversal of this order :

e.g. *When the bough breaks*, the cradle will fall.

Subordinate adverbial clause, qualifying verb *will fall* : *When the bough breaks*.

Exercise 158.—Point out the adverbial clauses of time in the following sentences :

1. We sank back exhausted after our guests had gone.
2. The telegram arrived before we had set off. 3. When the cat's away, the mice will play. 4. He has not darkened these doors again since Joshua kicked him downstairs. 5. I'll watch while you sleep. 6. Make me this promise ere I go. 7. As long as Mrs. Tittle-Tattle is alive there'll be no peace in this parish. 8. Till we meet, keep the secret dark. 9. As soon as the alarm was sounded, a cordon of police surrounded the house. 10. There was no rose in all the world until you came.

It must not be assumed that words such as *when* always introduce an adverbial clause of time.

Consider the following sentences :

(i) The waiting women wept for joy *when the missing trawlers returned to port.*

(ii) The day *when the missing trawlers returned to port* was old Mother Baxter's birthday.

E *

In each of these sentences there are two clauses :

Sentence (i) The waiting women wept for joy: Main Clause.

When the missing trawlers returned to port : Subordinate Adverbial Clause of Time, qualifying *wept*.

Sentence (ii) The day was Old Mother Baxter's birthday : Main Clause.

When the missing trawlers returned to port : Subordinate Adjectival Clause qualifying *day*.

The clause, *when the missing trawlers returned to port,* has exactly the same form as in the previous sentence but its function will be seen to be different.

In sentence (ii) it is qualifying a noun, *day.* It is therefore a subordinate adjectival clause qualifying the noun *day.*

In sentence (i) *when* is a subordinating conjunction.

In sentence (ii) *when* is a relative adverb :

Exercise 159.—State whether the clauses in italics are adverbial or adjectival :

1. *When the Smiths arrived* they seemed to bring their whole household effects with them. 2. The day *when the Smiths arrived* spelt tragedy for our home. 3. Can you tell me the time *when the train leaves for Rugby*? 4. There is usually a little room left in the compartment *when the train leaves for Rugby*. 5. *As the mist cleared,* we saw the snow-capped mountain cap gleaming before us. 6. We are climbing the same mountain *as the Swiss Alpine Club use for tests.*

2. *Adverbial Clauses of Place.*

Consider the following sentences :

   (i) The sleuth followed me *everywhere*.
   (ii) The sleuth followed me *wherever I went*.

In sentence (i) *everywhere* is an adverb of Place, answering the question *Where ?* It qualifies the verb *followed.*

In sentence (ii) *where I went* is a clause qualifying the verb *followed* and answering the question *Where ?* It is a

subordinate adverbial clause of Place qualifying verb
followed.

Sentence (i) would be analysed :

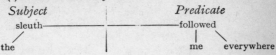

Sentence (ii) :

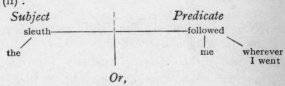

Or,

The sleuth followed me : Main Clause.

wherever I went : Subordinate Adverbial Clause of
Place qualifying verb *followed*.

Exercise 160.—Name the subordinate adverbial clauses
of place in the following :

1. He will stay where you leave him.   2. Wherever you
go, you will always remember Chalfont.   3. Where'er you
walk, cool vales shall fan the glade.   4. Whither I go,
thither ye cannot come.   5. They were walking now where
in days gone by Lady Peel had trod.

Exercise 161.—State whether the clauses in italics are
adverbial clauses of place or adjectival clauses :

1. *Where the bee sucks*, there suck I.   2. I remember the
house *where I was born*.   3. The intrepid moth-catcher
climbed *where no local inhabitant dared go*.   4. The ledge
where he is standing now is two hundred feet above the
shore.   5. The country *whence you travel* is shrouded in
mystery.   6. The town of Blantyre *where Livingstone was
born* is very proud of the achievements of the great explorer.

3. *Adverbial Clauses of Manner or Comparison.*

(*a*) Consider the following sentences :

    (i) The old man faced this new disaster *character-
       istically*.

(ii) The old man faced this new disaster *as you would have expected him to do.*

How did the old man face the new disaster ? *Characteristically. Characteristically* is, therefore, an adverb of manner. In sentence 2 the question, *How did the old man face the new disaster ?* is answered by the clause, *as you would have expected him to do.* This is then an adverbial clause of manner.

(*b*) Sometimes, where a comparison is explicit, the subordinate clause is called an adverbial clause of Comparison : e.g. He treats me better *than he treats you.*

(*c*) Consider the following sentence :

He plays golf as seriously *as he preaches his sermons.*

As seriously as he preaches his sermons answers the question " How seriously does he play golf ? " and so the clause is sometimes called *an adverbial clause of Degree,* qualifying the adverb *seriously.*

Exercise 162.—Point out the adverbial clauses of manner (comparison or degree) in the following :

1. Cleopatra died as she had lived, surrounded with pomp and splendour. 2. As we sow, so do we reap. 3. The old retired bank manager now keeps the books of the Village Institute as systematically as he did those in the branch office years ago. 4. The man is older than he appears to be. 5. The loss of life was less considerable than was at first supposed.

Correct Construction.

Which of the two following sentences is correct :

(i) *You love her more than me.*
(ii) *You love her more than I.*

Actually both can be correct, but they convey a different meaning.

The meaning of the first sentence is :
You love her more than (you love) me.

The meaning of the second sentence is :
You love her more than I (love her).

The case of the pronoun can best be determined by completing the sentence mentally. Not uncommonly we meet in colloquial English " He's older than me " for the more grammatically correct " He's older than I." But it must be remembered that *than* is a conjunction which does not govern a case.

Exercise 163.—Show the difference in meaning between the following pairs of sentences by mentally completing each sentence :

1. The Johnstons entertain their relatives more than we. The Johnstons entertain their relatives more than us. 2. The old lady will leave her housekeeper more money than I. The old lady will leave her housekeeper more money than me. 3. The butcher treats her better than I. The butcher treats her better than me.

4. *Adverbial Clauses of Reason or Cause.*

An adverbial clause of Time answers the question *When* ?
    We slept *until the reveillé sounded*.
An adverbial clause of Place answers the question *Where* ?
    We slept *where we could*.
An adverbial clause of Manner answers the question *How* ?
    We slept *as we deserved*.
A fourth adverbial clause answers the question *Why* ?
    We slept *because we were tired*.

This last clause is called a subordinate *adverbial clause of Reason or Cause.*

Adverbial clauses of reason can be introduced by (i) the subordinating conjunctions, *because, since, as, for,* etc. ; (ii) such phrases as *in that, seeing that.*

Exercise 164.—Pick out the adverbial clauses of reason in the following sentences :

1. We all dislike her because she puts on airs and graces. 2. Since you must know, he is on trial for embezzlement. 3. As it was late, we sported a taxi. 4. We were now in a sorry plight, for the petrol was running very low. 5. Seeing that you know everyone's business, perhaps you can tell me Smith's reason for leaving the factory. 6. I have sinned in that I have betrayed innocent blood.

Exercise 165.—(*a*) Construct eight sentences using the word *as* to introduce (i) two adjectival clauses; (ii) two adverbial clauses of time; (iii) two adverbial clauses of manner; (iv) two adverbial clauses of reason.

(*b*) Construct four sentences using the word *since* to introduce (i) two adverbial clauses of time; (ii) two adverbial clauses of reason.

Exercise 166.—Supply three adverbial clauses of time, place and reason that could be appropriately used to complete the following sentences :

1. Men must work . . .   2. The harvest was being gathered . . .   3. The children were having a gay time on the swings . . .   4. . . . the work of demolition was in progress.   5. . . . I shall put up for the night.

5. *Adverbial Clauses of Purpose.*

(i) Let us refer again to the four adverbial clauses at the head of the last section :

We slept
$$\begin{cases} \text{\textit{until the reveillé sounded.}} & \text{(Time.)} \\ \text{\textit{where we could.}} & \text{(Place.)} \\ \text{\textit{as we deserved.}} & \text{(Manner.)} \\ \text{\textit{because we were tired.}} & \text{(Reason.)} \end{cases}$$

Consider a fifth adverbial clause that gives the *purpose* of our sleeping, answering the question, *For what purpose have we slept ?*

We slept that *we might be ready for the battle of the morrow.*

The italicised clause is a subordinate adverbial clause of *purpose*, qualifying the verb *slept*. *That* is a subordinating conjunction. Other links that introduce a subordinate adverbial clause of purpose are : *so, that, in order that,* etc.

Exercise 167.—Complete the following sentences by supplying subordinate adverbial clauses of purpose (e.g. The student worked hard . . . (that he might pass the examination)) :

1. The young lady spent two hours before her mirror so that . . .   2. The doctor advised an X-ray in order

that . . . 3. Men worked that . . . 4. A man is always stationed at the bathing pool that . . . 5. The widow stinted herself that . . .

(ii) The negative form may be expressed in one of two ways :

    (a) Take heed that ye enter not into temptation ;

               Or,

    (b) Take heed *lest ye* enter into temptation.

Although the adverbial clause of purpose is frequently used, the use of the infinitive phrase to express purpose is commoner, probably because it is shorter :

e.g. The student worked hard to pass the examination. We dye to live. He works hard to keep body and soul together. I have come here today to invite you . . .

6. *Adverbial Clauses of Result.*

Consider the following sentence :

Aunt Sabina is so fat *that she can scarcely walk*.

The italicised clause indicates the *result of consequence* of Aunt Sabina's being so fat. Aunt Sabina is so fat *with the result that she.* . . .

These clauses state the consequence or result.

Exercise 168.—Name the adverbial clauses of consequence or result in the following sentences :

1. Buster eats so much that it costs a small fortune to keep him. 2. The assistant spoke so affectedly that the country folk could not understand her. 3. He has gone so far into crime that he could not easily retract. 4. It was now so dark that we had to feel our way. 5. The fire had now reached alarming proportions so that brigades from neighbouring towns had to be called. 6. A thick mist came down over the sea so that the enemy ships were able to make good their escape.

7. *Adverbial Clauses of Concession* are introduced by such subordinating conjunctions as : *though, even if, albeit,* etc.:

e.g. *Although he is wealthy* he is very humble.

    Though I speak with the tongues of men and of angels and have not love, I am nothing.

The subordinate clause expresses what is conceded or admitted. The concession is sometimes represented by an inversion without a conjunction :

e.g. *Be they of high or low estate*, Hobson has but one horse for hire.

Exercise 169.—Construct complex sentences by supplying appropriate main clauses to the following adverbial clauses of concession :

1. . . . although the sea was calm. 2. . . . though it was still early. 3. Although he is a wide reader . . . 4. Albeit the patient's temperature was lower . . . 5. Even if you are a busy man . . . 6. Be it wet or fine, . . . 7. Hungry as he was . . .

Exercise 170.—Construct four sentences with subordinate adverbial clauses introduced by *so that*, two to express *purpose*, and two to express *result*.

8. *Adverbial Clauses of Condition.*

(1) Consider the following sentence :
    If it rains, the meeting will be held indoors.

If it rains is called an adverbial clause of condition. It qualifies the verb *will be held*, stating *the conditions* under which the meeting will be held indoors. Adverbial clauses of condition are also introduced by :

(i) *unless : Unless you listen*, you cannot understand. (unless—if not.)

(ii) *provided that :* You will get better, *provided that you do not overdo it.*

(iii) *supposing : Supposing the hotel is full*, what do you propose doing ?

(iv) *on condition that :* You can attend the meeting *on condition that* you do not take part.

(2) Consider the following sentence :
    If I *were* you, I should agree to the terms.

The subordinate adverbial clause of condition *If I were you* represents a condition that is impossible to be fulfilled. It will be seen that the subjunctive mood is used.

In most conditional clauses the indicative mood is used, but when the condition is impossible to be fulfilled or unlikely to be fulfilled the subjunctive is used :

(i) If he *were* king instead of cobbler, he might be excused such pride.

(ii) If she *were* to return to us from her grave, she would rejoice to see us engaged in such work.

The unfulfilled condition may be expressed by means of an inversion : *Had we breathed a sound*, our presence would have been detected. Such conditions expressed in the subjunctive mood are sometimes called *Rejected Conditions*; others expressed in the indicative mood are called *Open Conditions*.

Exercise 171.—Pick out the adverbial clauses of condition in the following :

1. Speak clearly if you speak at all. 2. I could not have come if you had not supplied the fare. 3. Unless you stop, I shall fire. 4. Providing that you promise never to do it again, I will forgive you. 5. We were admitted to the ring-side seats on condition that no one else claimed the places. 6. Had you come when I telephoned, you might have saved him. 7. I'll be hanged if I'll be your serving-man.

Exercise 172.—What difference of meaning do you detect between the sentences in each of the following pairs :

1. If he has led a good, temperate life, there will be some hope for him. If he had led a good, temperate life, there would have been some hope for him. 2. If I can sing, I prefer to sing classical pieces. If I sang, I should prefer to sing classical pieces. 3. If the king knows our plans, we shall evoke his ill-pleasure. If the king should know our plans, we should evoke his ill-pleasure. 4. If I have a son, I shall be a good father to him. If I had a son, I should be a good father to him.

Exercise 173.—(Revision.) Pick out all the adverbial clauses in the following passages, stating (i) what kind they are, and (ii) what verbs they qualify :

An attempt was made in 1671 by a man named Captain Blood to steal the Crown jewels, which were kept in an iron cage in the Tower of London. As the only guard was over eighty, Blood thought it would be an easy task. Disguised as a clergyman, he made frequent visits to the Tower so that he could become friendly with the keeper. He was so successful that he persuaded the keeper to allow his daughter to marry Blood's " nephew." When the old man came into the Tower with his daughter for the wedding ceremony, he was seized and bound by four armed men. While one snatched at the crown, the others took possession of the orb and sceptre, but since the latter was too long to be carried inconspicuously, it was sawn into three parts. As they were busily engaged in stowing away the booty, the keeper's son came into the Tower. Although they could have overpowered the youth, the thieves ran out. As they were making their way across St. Catherine's Wharf, they were caught. If King Charles had listened to his advisers, he would have punished Blood and his accomplices with stern measures. He did not treat Blood as he deserved or banish him where other enemies of the State had been banished. As Blood had been disappointed in his venture he was given a grant of land in Ireland as a kind of compensation, provided he mended his ways.

C. Noun Clauses.

A clause can also do the work of a noun. A noun appears in different functions in the sentence in both subject and predicate, and a noun clause can similarly be used.

(a) *Noun Clauses in the Nominative.*

(i) As subject to a verb in the main clause :

e.g. (1) This military information must be known to the enemy.

(2) That we are to attack tomorrow must be known to the enemy.

In sentence (1) the noun *information* is the subject of *must be known*. In sentence (2) the noun equivalent is the clause *that we are to attack tomorrow*. The clause is, therefore, a noun clause, subject to the verb *must be known* in the main clause.

The sentence should be analysed graphically :

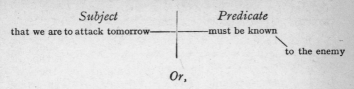

Subject	*Predicate*
that we are to attack tomorrow———————	—must be known
	to the enemy

Or,

must be known to the enemy : Main Clause.
we are to attack tomorrow : Subordinate Noun Clause,
   subject to verb *must be known.*
that : a link, a subordinating conjunction.

Exercise 174.—Supply noun clauses as subjects to the
following (e.g. . . . is no concern of hers (Noun Subject
Clause, What I wear)) :

1. . . . is one of the present Mayor's greatest achievements. 2. . . . came as a great surprise to us. 3. . . . is a
well-known saying. 4. . . . was the unanimous verdict.
5. . . . was received as bad news by the townsfolk.

(ii) Noun subject clause in apposition to the subject :

e.g. (1) The fact that his licence had never been pre-
      viously endorsed may be to his advantage.

The fact may be to his advantage : Main Clause.
that his licence has never been previously endorsed :
   Subordinate Noun Clause in apposition to noun *fact.*

Contrast the foregoing sentence :

    (2) The fact *that we must not forget* is the possibility
       of a surprise attack.

In sentence (1), *that his licence had never been previously
endorsed* is in apposition to *fact* and is a subordinate *noun*
clause. *That* is a subordinating conjunction.

In sentence (2), *that we must not forget* is an adjectival
clause qualifying the noun *fact.* It is thus an *adjectival*
clause qualifying noun *fact.* *That* is a relative pronoun.

If you find any difficulty in distinguishing between

adjectival and noun clauses in apposition, try to substitute another form of the relative pronoun (e.g. who, whom, which). If this is possible, the clause must be adjectival.

Exercise 175.—State whether the italicised subordinate clauses in the following sentences are noun clauses in apposition or adjectival clauses :

1. The announcement *that the Prime Minister was in America* caused considerable excitement. 2. The announcement *that was received last night* caused considerable excitement. 3. The fact *that I was present at the accident* does not make me responsible for it. 4. The fact *which you have to face* is that you are now penniless. 5. The news *that was broadcast* was received with much enthusiasm. 6. The news *that the King was to visit the Midlands* was received with much enthusiasm.

(iii) Noun clauses used predicatively (as complements of the subject) :

> e.g. (1) The beggar was a fraud.
> (2) The beggar was not what he pretended.

The noun *fraud* is used predicatively to complete the sense of the verb in sentence (1).
what he pretended is a clause, used as an equivalent of a noun in the complement :

The beggar was not : Main Clause.
what he pretended : Subordinate Noun Clause used predicatively with the verb *was not*.

Exercise 176.—Supply noun clauses used predicatively (as complements of the subject) in the following (e.g. My claim is . . . (My claim is that *the cyclist was carrying no rear light*)) :

1. The opinion of the judge was . . . 2. The advice of the lawyer was . . . 3. The decision of the Tribunal is . . . 4. The schoolboy has not turned out . . . 5. Life, after all, is . . .

(b) *Noun Clauses in the Accusative.*

(i) Noun clauses as object to verb in main clauses.

Consider the following sentences :

(1) The foreman of the jury announced the verdict.
(2) The foreman of the jury announced that the prisoner
was guilty.

The clause *that the prisoner was guilty* takes the place
of the noun *verdict*, which is the object of the verb
announced.

that the prisoner was guilty is, therefore, a noun clause,
object to the verb *announced* in the main clause.

The analysis would be :

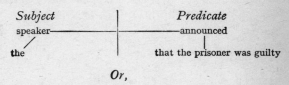

Subject	*Predicate*
speaker—————	—————announced
the	that the prisoner was guilty

Or,

The speaker announced : Main Clause.
the prisoner was guilty : Subordinate Noun Clause, object
of verb *announced*.
that : a link, a subordinating conjunction.

Exercise 177.—Supply noun clauses as objects to the following (e.g. The police discovered ... (*that the library window
had been left unlatched*)) :

1. The chairman of the Building Society reported that ...
2. The waiter replied that . . . 3. We at last found
that . . . 4. Have you ever realised that . . . 5. Don't
tell me that . . . 6. Tell me . . .

The Direct Quotation.

Pope said, " The proper study of Mankind is man."
It looks as if the direct quotation is the direct object of
the verb *said*, and is a noun object clause. But, as the
quotation marks indicate, " The ... man " is separate from
the structure of the sentence. It is preferable, therefore,
to regard the quotation as another main clause. If the
sentence is rendered in indirect speech, *Pope said that the
proper study of mankind was man,* the clause *the proper*

study of mankind was man is part of the framework of the sentence and is therefore a noun clause, object of the verb *said*.

(ii) Noun clause in apposition to a noun in the accusative :

e.g. The wretched people now appreciated the fact that *they had been deserted*.

Main Clause : *The wretched people now appreciated the fact.*
Subordinate Noun Clause in apposition to noun in accusative : *that they had been deserted*.

The subordinate clause is in apposition to the noun *fact*, which is the object of the verb *appreciated*.

Exercise 178.—Supply noun clauses in apposition to the objects in the following sentences (*N.B.*—Be careful not to give adjectival clauses) :

1. The prisoner heard the charge that . . . 2. The employees lodged their grievance that . . . 3. The explorers realised the ghastly mistake that . . . 4. The school has the motto that . . . 5. We came across the theory that . . .

(iii) The noun clause as object of a transitive verb of incomplete predication.

Consider the following sentence :

Her hard life has made her a cynic.

The word *cynic* completes the meaning of the verb *made* and is in agreement with *her*, the object of *made*.

Instead of the noun *cynic*, a clause could be used :

e.g. Her hard life has made her *what you would expect*.

What you would expect is a noun object clause, object of the transitive verb of incomplete predication, *make*.

Exercise 179.—Supply the noun object clauses in the following :

1. You may call me . . . 2. The shock has rendered her . . . 3. I shall make my son . . . 4. His followers created him . . .

(iv) A noun object clause as object to a preposition. Consider :

(a) The Under Secretary had nothing to add to his previous statement.

Statement is the accusative case following the preposition *to*.

(b) The Under Secretary had nothing to add *to what he had said previously on this subject.*

The clause in italics is a noun object clause, object of the preposition *to*.

Exercise 180.—Supply noun clauses as objects to the prepositions in the following sentences :

1. His friend is different from . . . 2. Nothing can detract from . . . 3. Your achievement cannot be compared with . . . 4. I have nothing to say against . . . 5. I cannot vouch for his statement beyond . . .

Exercise 181.—Pick out subordinate noun clauses in the following passages, stating their kind and function :

1. Five friends decided that they would travel by train from Cambridge to London. 2. One of them, Wiggins, placed his railway ticket in his hatband. 3. The fact that it was a drowsy afternoon sent one of the five off to sleep. 4. What happened next constitutes one of the most amusing episodes of the London to Cambridge line. 5. When they heard that the collector was approaching, they removed the ticket from his hatband. 6. They awoke the sleeper, who discovered that he had lost his ticket. 7. His friends asked him what he was going to do to avoid a second payment of fare. 8. What Wiggins suggested was the sharing of the cost amongst the five. 9. The other four were not impressed by what Wiggins suggested. 10. One of them had the bright idea that Wiggins should hide under the seat. 11. He decided that this was the best scheme. 12. That it was also a dirty one was apparent later on. 13. The four friends gave the collector five tickets. 14. The collector's remark was what might have been expected. 15. He asked why there were five tickets

for four people.   16. The four friends then revealed where their friend was hiding.   17. " It seems that he prefers travelling under the seat," commented the collector.

D. CLAUSES—*Noun, Adjectival, Adverbial*.

It is not the form but the function of a clause that determines whether it is a Noun, Adjectival or Adverbial Clause. Consider the clause : *when we saw the sun rise*.

This clause can be used as a noun, an adjectival clause or an adverbial clause : e.g.

1. I shall never forget *when we saw the sun rise*.
    when we saw the sun rise : Noun Clause, object to verb *shall forget*.
2. We struck tents *when we saw the sun rise*.
    when we saw the sun rise : Adverbial Clause of Time to verb *struck* in main clause.
3. The morning *when we saw the sun rise* was the last we spent in Egypt.
    when we saw the sun rise : Adjectival Clause qualifying the noun *morning*.

Exercise 182.—Construct sentences using the following in three ways : (i) as noun clauses ; (ii) as adjectival clauses ; (iii) as adverbial clauses.

1. where we are going ; 2. when they left ; 3. that you eat.

Exercise 183.—Pick out a noun clause, an adjectival clause and an adverbial clause in each of the following sentences :

1. When the holiday was over, the tourists who had enjoyed their cruise told the guide that it had been a most instructive and healthy month.   2. Lest you forget again, I must remind you that parcels which are not claimed within three months are despatched to the Head Office. 3. Unless you are seeking a quarrel with a man whom you ought to respect, the fact that you are penniless ought to influence your action a little.   4. Wherever you go, you will never find a man who is readier to forgive what other people would regard as unpardonable insults.

Revision

1. What do you understand by the following terms :

   (i) a phrase ; (ii) a clause ; (iii) a simple sentence
   with a double subject ; (iv) a double sentence ;
   (v) an elliptical sentence ; (vi) a multiple sentence ;
   (vii) a complex sentence ?

2. Each of the following is an example of one of the six
word-groups mentioned in (1). Classify them.

   (i) When the last colonial soldier goes away, the streets
       will be all lined with the girls he left behind.
  (ii) Off with his head.
 (iii) After the ball is over.
  (iv) He called and knocked but no one came.
   (v) Into the jaws of death.
  (vi) Jack and Jill went up the hill to fetch a pail of water.

3. Construct sentences to illustrate

   Adverbial Clause of Time.
   ,,   ,,   Place.
   ,,   ,,   Manner or Comparison.
   ,,   ,,   Reason or Cause.
   ,,   ,,   Purpose.
   ,,   ,,   Result.
   ,,   ,,   Condition.

4. When is the Subjunctive Mood used in English ?

5. Construct sentences to illustrate :

   (i) A Noun Object Clause.
  (ii) A Noun Subject Clause.
 (iii) A Noun Clause used predicatively.

CHAPTER XIII

HOW TO ANALYSE A SENTENCE

I. Complex Sentences

So far in this book sentences have been analysed by what is called the Graphic Analysis method. By this method we can see at a glance the construction of the simple sentence, the subject and its enlargements, the verb and its enlargements, the object and its enlargements. When we come to deal with complex, double and multiple sentences we meet with longer and involved sentences. It is recommended that these longer sentences be divided into clauses in a tabular method as will be shown, and each clause, if required, analysed in a detailed manner by the graphic method.

In *Clause Analysis*, the sentence is divided into its component clauses: the kind of each clause is indicated, its function in the sentence, its relationship to other clauses in the sentence.

In *Detailed Analysis*, as has already been noted, each clause is divided into its constituent parts and the relationship shown.

How to Analyse a Sentence.

The following method is suggested in analysing a sentence:

Step 1. Name the *finite* verb. There will be a clause, main or subordinate, for each verb.

Step 2. Name each of the clauses. Remember that sometimes one clause breaks into the middle of another: e.g. The girl, *who rather fancied herself*, was dressed in a most extravagant manner.

Step 3. Notice signs for co-ordinate clauses or subordinate clauses; look for conjunctions, relative pronouns, relative adverbs, etc.

Step 4. Determine the main clause or clauses.

Step 5. Decide what the relationship between the clauses is. Examine each subordinate clause in turn. Relate each to its main clause. Is it a noun, adjectival or adverbial clause ?

Step 6. Set out the analysis in tabular form as shown.

Step 7. State the kind of sentence : Complex, Double, Multiple.

Step 8. (If required) Analyse each individual clause graphically.

EXAMPLE 1. After the rain had ceased, the party went for a brisk walk to Hangman's Hill, which has a commanding view of the estuary.

Step 1. Finite verbs : *had ceased, went, has.*

Step 2. There are three clauses, one for each of the finite verbs :

After the rain had ceased,
the party went for a brisk walk to Hangman's Hill,
which has a commanding view of the estuary.

Step 3. Links : *After* (conjunction), *which* (relative pronoun).

Step 4. *The party went for a walk* : Main Clause.

Step 5. *After* . . . introducing Adverbial Clause of Time.
which . . . introducing Adjectival Clause.

Step 6. The Tabulated Analysis.

No.	Clause	Link	Kind	Function
A	The party went for a walk to Hangman's Hill		Main Clause	Independent.
a^1	the rain had ceased	after	Subord. Adverbial Clause of Time	Qualifying verb *went* in A.
a^2	which has a commanding view of the estuary		Subord. Adjectival Clause	Qualifying noun *Hill* in A.

Notice that *after* is a conjunction and is not part of the structure of the clause a^1 ; *which* is a link, but as a relative pronoun has a function in the sentence, subject of verb *has*.

The numbering arrangement suggested is that main clauses are numbered in capitals, their subordinate clauses in corresponding small letters.

Step 7. The sentence is Complex.
Step 8. Detailed Analysis (if required).

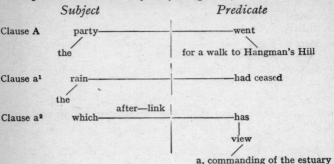

	Subject		*Predicate*
Clause A	party—————————went
	the /		for a walk to Hangman's Hill
Clause a¹	rain—————————had ceased
	the /
Clause a²	which————————has
	after—link		view
			a, commanding of the estuary

EXAMPLE 2. Wherever we went, the hotel-keepers
regretfully informed us that all their rooms were engaged.

Step 1. Finite verbs : *went, informed, were engaged.*
Step 2. There are three clauses :
> *we went,*
> *the hotel-keepers regretfully informed us,*
> *all their rooms were engaged.*

Step 3. Links : *wherever* (conjunction), *that* (conjunction).
Step 4. *The hotel-keepers regretfully informed us* : Main
Clause.
Step 5. *wherever . . .* introducing Adverbial Clause of Place.
that . . . introducing Noun Object Clause.
Step 6. The Tabulated Analysis :

No.	Clause	Link	Kind	Function
A	The hotel-keepers regretfully in-formed us		Main Clause	Independent.
a¹	we went	wherever	Subord. Adverbial Clause of Place	Qualifying verb *informed* in A.
a²	all their rooms were engaged	that	Subord. Noun Cl.	Direct Obj. of verb *informed* in A.

Step 7. The sentence is Complex.
Step 8. Detailed Analysis (if required).

EXAMPLE 3.   Although the strikers, who were led by a young fanatic named Mizen, knew what serious consequences to the nation might result from their action, they persisted in their demands until an arbitration court was established.

Step 1. Finite verbs : *were led, knew, might result, persisted, was established.*

Step 2. There are five clauses :
> *The strikers knew,*
> *who were led by a young fanatic named Mizen,*
> *what serious consequences to the nation might result from their action,*
> *they persisted in their demands,*
> *an arbitration court was established.*

Step 3. Links : *although, until.*

Step 4. *They persisted in their demands* : Main Clause.

Step 5. *Although the strikers . . . knew :* Adverbial Clause of Concession.
> *who . . .* introducing Adjectival Clause.
> *what serious consequences . . .* introducing Noun Object Clause.
> *until . . .* introducing Adverbial Clause of Time.

Step 6. The Tabulated Analysis :

No.	Clause	Link	Kind	Function
A	They persisted in their demands		Main	Independent.
a¹	the strikers knew	although	Subord. Adverbial Cl. of Concession	Qualifying verb *persisted* in A.
a²	who were led by a young fanatic named Mizen		Subord. Adject. Clause	Qualifying noun *strikers* in a¹.
a³	what serious consequences to the nation might result from this action		Subord. Noun Cl.	Object to verb *knew* in a¹.
a⁴	an arbitration court was established	until	Subord. Adverbial Clause of Time	Qualifying verb *persisted* in A.

N.B.—Note that one clause (a²) is subordinate to another subordinate clause (a¹).

Step 7. It is a Complex Sentence.

Step 8. Detailed Analysis (if required).

Exercise 184.—Analyse the following complex sentences into clauses in the manner shown. Steps 1-5 should be followed mentally. Only the tabulated form of the analysis should be written (Step 6). Detailed analysis of individual clauses is not required.

1. Daniel Defoe, who wrote the Journal of the Plague Year, records an interesting incident which occurred at his brother's warehouse.   2. Whilst he was walking in Swan Alley, he saw a woman coming out of the warehouse with some high-crowned hats.   3. She told him that there were other people inside the warehouse.   4. The fact that many people were leaving the warehouse with hats made him so suspicious that he went inside.   5. When he had shut the gate behind him, he asked the women what they were doing there.   6. The truth was that they were seizing hats from the warehouse, which apparently had no owner.   7. They thought that they might take possession of them as no one else was there to claim them.   8. They were unconcerned and quiet as if they had been at a hatter's shop buying for their money.

Exercise 185.—Combine the following groups of sentences to form complex sentences (this process, the opposite to Analysis, is called Synthesis) (e.g. You are the rogue. You stole my bicycle.—You are the rogue who stole my bicycle) :

1. Parliament is opened by the King at the beginning of each session. The King outlines the schemes which will be discussed by Parliament.   2. Representatives are elected to Parliament by the people. They come from every district of the United Kingdom.   3. The debates are under the control of the Speaker. He is supposed to present the decisions of Parliament to the King.   4. The policy of the Government is directed by the Prime Minister. He is assisted by the Cabinet. Each member of the Cabinet is responsible for one State Department. Any question can be asked in the House concerning one of these departments.

II. Double and Multiple Sentences

Double and Multiple sentences are a series of two or more main clauses which are linked together. The clauses are of equal importance ; one is not grammatically subordinate to the other :

e.g. We knocked twice, but no one came. (Double Sentence.)

The two clauses are co-ordinate. They are both main clauses ; neither is dependent upon the other. The two co-ordinate clauses are linked by the conjunction *but*, which is called a *Co-ordinating Conjunction*. The steps in the clause analysis of a Double or Multiple Sentence are the same as in a Complex Sentence.

The clause analysis of the sentence given above would be :

No.	Clause	Link	Kind	Function
A	We knocked twice		Main	Co-ord. with B.
B	No one came	but	Main	Co-ord. with A.

Kind—Double

Sentence 2.   I came, I saw, I conquered.

No.	Clause	Kind	Function
A	I came	Main	Co-ord. with B and C.
B	I saw	Main	Co-ord. with A and C.
C	I conquered	Main	Co-ord. with A and B.

Kind—Multiple

Sentence 3.   The gale tore up fences and uprooted trees. There are two finite verbs in this sentence and therefore two clauses.

The noun *gale* is subject to both verbs.

Analysis :

No.	Clause	Link	Kind	Function
A	The gale tore up fences		Main	Co-ord. with B.
B	(The gale) uprooted trees	and	Main	Co-ord. with A.

Kind—Double

Similarly the two verbs might share one object.

Sentence 4.   I neither respect nor trust him.

No.	Clause	Link	Kind	Function
A	I respect (him)	neither	Main	Co-ord. with B.
B	(I) trust him	nor	Main	Co-ord. with A.

Kind—Double

The co-ordinate main clauses in a Double or Multiple sentence may themselves have clauses subordinate to them.

Sentence 5.   When the storm was at its height, the gale tore up the fences and uprooted trees which had proudly resisted wind and weather for many years.

No.	Clause	Link	Kind	Function
A	The gale tore up the fences		Main	Co-ord. with B.
a¹	the storm was at its height	when	Subord. Adverbial Clause of Time	Qualifying verb *tore* in A.
B	(the gale) uprooted trees	and	Main	Co-ord. with A.
b¹	which had proudly resisted wind and weather for many years		Subord. Adjectival Clause	Qualifying noun *trees* in B.

Kind—Double

In other words, the Double sentence is made up of two co-ordinate complex sentences.

Exercise 186.—Analyse the following double and multiple sentences into clauses :

1. Mother chose the dress but Father paid the bill.   2. I asked no questions but her chatter soon gave the game away.   3. Either you must work harder or you will fail your examination.   4. The recruit was first interviewed by the sergeant, who passed him on to a lieutenant.   5. We rowed and fished all the day but no luck came our way.

6. I may know and trust the young man but he would not be my choice for you. 7. Father, who makes an excellent Santa Claus, entertained the children and distributed the gifts. 8. After the game was over, the team returned to the home town and received a civic welcome because they had brought the cup to the town for the first time.

III. Final Notes on Analysis

Clause analysis is not merely a mechanical and artificial exercise. The man who treats his car most carefully is the man who knows exactly how it works. He knows why it is unwise to drive off at a high speed immediately after the car has been started up on a cold day. He knows why it is better to have a silent gear change.

Practice in the analysis of sentences can develop an appreciation of the well-constructed sentence and assist in detecting the faults of a loose sentence. It takes you into the workshop of the language. You see how the sentence works.

After you have completed the exercises in analysis given below, take a passage from a leader in the daily paper and analyse each of the sentences in the way you have been shown.

These additional points should be noted:

1. The following are not part of the grammatical construction of a sentence:

   (i) Conjunctions.   They *join* and are not part of clauses.
  (ii) Interjections.   E.g. Hurrah ! we have won.
 (iii) Vocatives.

2. Certain anticipatory or introductory words cause difficulty.

   (i) E.g. *There* was a crooked man.

There does not state where the crooked man was. You will notice that in saying the sentence aloud the word *there* has a little emphasis. It almost has the function of anticipating the subject.

Perhaps it is as well to regard *there* as an adverb of place, although all its significance has gone.

F

(ii) E.g. It is fortunate that we have our torches with us.

The sentence might read : *That we have our torches with us is fortunate.* But this is a little clumsy and, probably owing to the desire to construct a sentence in the common order of subject followed by predicate, the custom has arisen to introduce an introductory *it*.

It is possible to regard *that we have our torches with us* as a noun clause in apposition to *it*.

(iii) A non-finite part of the verb may govern a subordinate clause.

> E.g. Fearing that his sheep might be carried away in the flood, the old shepherd folded them in the upper meadow.

The present participle *fearing*, which qualifies the noun *shepherd*, has as direct object *that his sheep might be carried away in the flood*.

Analysis :

No.	Clause	Link	Kind	Function
A	The old shepherd fearing folded them in the upper meadow		Main Clause	Independent.
a	his sheep might be carried away in the flood	that	Subord. Noun Clause	Object to participle *fearing* in A.

Complex Sentence

Exercise 187.—Analyse the following sentences into clauses :

1. Men may come, and men may go, But I go on for ever.   2. The Mayor was dumb and the Council stood, as if they were changed into blocks of wood.   3. A man once declared that he could lift himself into the air but his friends ridiculed the idea.   4. Green and blue his sharp eyes twinkled, like a candle flame when salt is sprinkled.   5. The hunters discovered that the fox, whom they had now been pursuing for four hours, had made for Hinchlea woods where probably it could run to earth.   6. Unless I hear from you by return of post, my assumption will be that

you have refused the offer because it is not generous enough.   7. Her finger was so small, the ring would not stay on, which they did bring.   8. I don't go much on religion, I never ain't had no show, but I've got a middlin' tight grip on the handful o' things I know.   9. I spake in a whisper, as he who speaks in a room where someone is lying dead, but he made no answer to what I said. 10. What he gives thee, see thou keep ; stay not thou for food or sleep, be it scroll or be it book ; into it, Knight, thou must not look.   11. At Charing Cross, hard by the way where we (thou know'st) do sell our hay, there is a house with stairs ; and there did I see coming down such folk as are not in our town, forty at least in pairs.   12. We did much as we chose to do ; we'd never heard of Mrs. Grundy ; all the theology we knew was that we mightn't play on Sunday.   13. That day a blizzard overtook them with such violence that, when they had marched for half an hour, Scott, realising that no one of them could face such weather, pitched camp and stayed there until the weather improved.   14. Unless he very quickly mends his ways, Master John will become what his father was before him and the Court will treat him as severely as it did his father.

15.   Snug in my easy chair, I stirred the fire to flame,
      I shut my eyes to heat and light
      And saw, in sudden night,
      Crouched in the dripping dark,
      With steaming shoulders stark,
      The man who hews the coal to feed my fire.

16. Her tongue was not less keen than her eye, and, whenever a damsel came within earshot, seemed to take up an unfinished lecture, as a barrel-organ takes up a tune, precisely at the point where it had left off.   17. The albatross was undisturbed for some time, until the noise of our bows, gradually approaching, roused him, when, lifting his head, he stared upon us for a moment, and then spread his wide wings and took his flight.   18. The rumour that the Prime Minister was to resign had become so widespread that it was being discussed in every village in England.   19. Finding that his first quest was in vain, the dealer then

approached the farmer who he hoped would sell some of his pedigree herd which was the pride of the district. 20. When he arrives where the horses are to be changed, he throws down the reins with something of an air and abandons the cattle to the care of an hostler, as his duty is merely to drive from one stage to another.

Revision

Read the following passage and answer the questions underneath :

No one can predict, no one can even imagine, how this terrible war against German and Nazi *aggression* will run its course or how *far* it will spread or how long it *will last*. Long, dark months of trials and tribulations lie before us. Not only great dangers but many *more* misfortunes, many shortcomings, many mistakes, many disappointments will surely be our lot.   Death and sorrow will be the companions of our journey, hardship *our* garment, constancy and valour our only shield.   We must be united, we must be undaunted, we must be inflexible.   Our qualities and deeds must burn and glow *through* the gloom of Europe *until* they become the inevitable *beacon* of its salvation.

(*a*) Analyse each of the sentences in the passage into its constituent clauses, showing their relationship.

(*b*) Parse the words in italics.

CHAPTER XIV

PUNCTUATION AND USE OF CAPITALS

WE are all obliged from time to time to listen to the speaker who gabbles at a considerable speed and in a breathless manner. When he pauses in his speech, usually with an undignified gulp, it is only to allow another intake of breath before he pours forth another torrent of sentences. There is, on the other hand, the opposite to this human whirlwind, whose pauses are both frequent and long. For example :

" And—er—now, Mr. Chairman,—er—I must—er, I must ask you—er—to consider another—er—point, which, in my view, in my—er—humble view—er—illustrate the—er—if I may be allowed the expression—the ineptitude—er—er—of the present—er—Government. The—er—Ministry of—er—Food—advertisement has—er—stated that an—er—egg—an egg, without the shell, that is, is three-quarters water, and that—er—only the—er—water is—er—taken out in making—it—er—into dried egg. Er—then,—er—Mr. Chairman, it goes on to—er—say—that one—er—tablespoon of dried egg with—er—two tablespoonfuls of—er—water—equals one egg. I suggest—er—that this—er—illustrates—the mathematical—er—unsoundness of—er—Her Majesty's Government."

Mr. Whirlwind's failure as a speaker is due to an absence of appropriate pauses. The critic of the Government failed as a speaker owing to a surfeit of them. In speaking, one's meaning is made clear and effective by the correct grouping of words together. The groups are distinguished by the pauses.

There are, of course, other ways besides the pause that make speech effective. There is the emphasis that can be imparted by the inflexions of the voice. Mr. Winston Churchill's occasional lifting of his voice at the end of a sentence, his pause before a particularly forceful adjective.

are known to all and have found many imitators. There are, then, other devices for securing emphasis in speech, but the pause is one that all of us employ regularly and quite naturally. The pause in speaking has its counterpart in writing in the *Stop*.

In the earliest writing, as has been shown earlier in this book, there were no divisions between words, let alone divisions between groups of words. The Greek grammarians divided groups of words by *points*. One group of words they called a *Colon*, which means " a limb " ; another group they called a *Comma*, which means " a piece cut off " ; another group, a whole sentence, they called a *Period*.

These words, *period, comma, colon*, are still used in English, but refer no longer to the groups of words but to the *points* or *stops* which separate them. This system of using points to assist the meaning of words is called Punctuation.

The student, therefore, should regard punctuation not as a set code of rules but as a means of ensuring that a passage is so divided that the meaning of the various parts and that of the whole is clear and unambiguous. Incorrect punctuation can convey an altogether wrong and sometimes ludicrous meaning. The time-honoured example of this is, of course, " Charles I walked and talked half an hour after his head was cut off."

In the *Midsummer Night's Dream*, Peter Quince, the carpenter, takes the part of the prologue when Bottom and his friends play their interlude before Duke Theseus on his wedding day. After he has said his opening piece, his noble listeners make gentle criticism :

THESEUS.   This fellow doth not stand upon points.

LYSANDER.   He hath rid his prologue like a rough colt ; he knows not the stop. A good moral, my lord—it is not enough to speak ; but to speak true.

HIPPOLYTA.   Indeed he hath played on his prologue like a child on a recorder—a sound but not in government.

THESEUS.   His speech was like a tangled chain ; nothing impaired, but all disordered.

It is worth while, then, giving a little attention to " the points."

In one of the earliest English pre-Shakespearean comedies, *Ralph Roister Doister*, the hero, Ralph, asks a scrivener to prepare a love-letter for the lady of his affection, Dame Christian Custance, an attractive widow. The letter is prepared and is eventually read by Matthew Merrygreek to the lady.   To her amazement and horror the overtures of love are expressed in far from endearing tones.

Ralph is highly indignant that he has been so badly let down and takes the letter back to the scrivener, who declares the letter was in order.   He says :

" Then was it as ye prayed to have it, I wot
But in reading and *pointing*, there was made some fault."

Merrygreek had put an altogether different interpretation on the passage by the incorrect pointing or punctuation. Then the scrivener re-read it with the correct pointing.

This is Merrygreek's punctuation.   Re-read the passage with the scrivener's punctuation.

Sweet mistress where as I love you nothing at all,
Regarding your substance and riches chief of all,
For your personage, beauty, demeanour and wit
I commend me unto you never a whit
Sorry to hear report of your good welfare.
For (as I hear say) such your conditions are,
That ye be worthy favour of no living man,
To be abhorred of every honest man.
And now by these presents I do advertise
That I am minded to marry you in no wise,
For your goodes and substances, I could be content
To take you as ye are.   If ye mind to be my wife
Ye shall be assured for the time of my life
I will keep you right well from good rayment and fare.
Ye shall not be kept but in sorrow and care.
Ye shall in no wise live at your own liberty.
Do and say what ye please, ye shall never please me,
But when ye are merry, I will be all sad.
When ye are sorry, I will be very glad.

Exercise 188.—Show how the meaning may be altered by a change in the punctuation of the following :

1. Wanted—for small country house a general to wash iron and dust daily.
2. " The foreman," said the works manager, " does not know his job."
3.   Every lady in this land
           Hath twenty nails upon each hand
           Five and twenty on hands and feet
           And this is true without deceit.
4. The policeman says the burglar is the plague of his life.
5. He was fighting furiously for his life ten seconds after a dagger pierced his heart.

The Marks of Punctuation

These must now be considered separately.

The Full Stop or *Period.*—(*a*) Its chief use is to show that the sentence is finished.

        Ben Battle was a soldier bold
        And used to war's alarms :
        But a cannon ball took off his legs
        So he laid down his arms.—Hood.

When the sentence is finished, be careful to put a full stop and start your next sentence with a capital letter.

Exercise 189.—Each of the following passages is made up of two or three sentences. Put in the full stops to mark the end of the sentences in each passage :

(i)   For he might have been a Roosian
         A French, or Turk or Proosian
             Or perhaps Ital-ian
         But in spite of all temptations
         To belong to other nations
         He remains an Englishman
                                   W. S. Gilbert.

(ii) When I was a lad I served a term
     As office boy to an Attorney's firm

I cleaned the windows and I swept the floor
And I polished up the handle of the big front door
I polished up that handle so carefulee
That now I am the Ruler of the Queen's Navee

Ibid.

(*b*) The full stop is also used to indicate abbreviations : e.g.

The Rt. Hon. Ernest Bevin, M.P., addressed the workers on Nov. 24th, at 8.15 p.m.

When this stop is used for abbreviation it may require to be followed by a comma : e.g.

The Vicar, the Rev. O. B. Glum, B.A., presided.

But a full stop indicating an abbreviation does not require another if it appears at the end of a sentence : e.g.

The motion was carried nem. con.

Exercise 190.—Supply ten common forms of abbreviation.

The Comma.—The sense of the passage will usually suggest when a comma is necessary. It is used :

(*a*) To separate a word, phrase or clause.

    (i) *Women are, generally speaking, more interested in clothes than men.*

    (ii) *The thief, who had slipped away in the crowd, was the richer by several thousand pounds.*

    (iii) *Lord, behold us met together.*

(*b*) To mark a series of words, phrases or clauses :

    So munch on, crunch on, take your nuncheon,
    Breakfast, supper, dinner, luncheon.

If *and* is inserted before the last item the comma is frequently omitted : e.g.

    To love, honour and obey.

(*c*) When an inversion of the normal order is used for emphasis : e.g.

    She received her guests without a smile,
but   *Without a smile, she received her guests.*

F *

(*d*) Before a direct quotation : e.g.

The Duke of Buckingham said, " The world is made up for the most part of fools and knaves."

(*e*) On any occasion where its presence simplifies the meaning : e.g.

The lady was accompanied by her husband and two dogs on leads.

To insert a comma after *husband* avoids an unpleasant interpretation of the sentence.

Exercise 191.—Insert commas and full stops where you think they are needed in the following. (*N.B.*—To insert a comma where it is not required is as incorrect as to omit it where it is required.)

1. Sir Boyle Roche who is credited with some most incredible statements is reputed to have said " Simple misfortunes never come alone and the greatest of all possible misfortunes is generally followed by a much greater "

2. Uncle Jeremy is always saying the wrong thing quite recently at a wedding ceremony where he was to propose the toast of the bride and bridegroom he remarked to the amazement of everyone that he had noticed that there had been more women than men married recently unfortunately he could not see anything incorrect in what he had said

The colon is denoted by (:). It separates a longer *limb* of the sentence than the comma. It is used only rarely now in English and many writers do without it altogether. It is used :

(*a*) To introduce a series : e.g.

Dickens wrote many novels, some of the most important of which are as follows : " David Copperfield," " Oliver Twist," " A Tale of Two Cities," " Martin Chuzzlewit " and " Pickwick Papers."

(*b*) To introduce a quotation : e.g.

When I recall his earlier devotion to our cause and his subsequent betrayal, how often I think of Browning's lines :

> Just for a handful of silver he left us ;
> Just for a riband to stick in his coat.

(*c*) A more subtle use of the colon is when it ends a sentence which is going to be amplified or developed in the next : e.g.

  (i) No higher praise can a man be paid than this : he was a man.
  (ii) Mary is not fit to be responsible for the discipline of the company : she is not disciplined herself.

The semi-colon is, perhaps, more important. It is not a pause like the comma but a stop, yet not a complete stop like the full stop. It breaks up a long sentence into smaller sentences that are complete in themselves from a grammatical point of view but are linked by reason of the similarity of subject-matter.

Examine the following :

" A friend of mine," said Lord Erskine, " was suffering from a continual wakefulness ; various methods were tried to send him to sleep, but in vain. At last his physicians resorted to an experiment which succeeded perfectly : they dressed him in a watchman's coat, put a lantern into his hand, placed him in a sentry-box and—he was asleep in ten minutes."

This little episode illustrates the difference in use of the comma, the colon and the semi-colon.

The semi-colon breaks up the long sentence, *A friend of mine . . . vain*. The two sentences separated by the semi-colon deal with the same subject-matter—the sleeplessness of Lord Erskine. There follows then a sentence beginning *At last his physicians . . .* and ending with *perfectly*, which is followed by a colon because the sentence to follow amplifies or explains the experiment. You then have a series of clauses separated by commas. The clauses all refer to the same subject, *he*, and the commas provide the link.

Exercise 192.—You are given the full stops in the following passage. Supply any commas, colons or semicolons you judge necessary :

The Tool-using Animal

But on the whole man is a tool-using animal. Weak in himself and of small stature he is the feeblest of bipeds. Three quintals are a crushing load for him the steer of the meadow tosses him about like a waste rag. Nevertheless he can use tools can devise tools with these the granite mountain melts into light dust before him he kneads glowing iron as if it were soft paste seas are his smooth highway winds and fire his unwearying steeds. Nowhere do you find him without tools without tools he is nothing with tools he is all.—CARLYLE.

The Mark of Interrogation (?)
   (*a*) " Did ever you see such a thing in your life ? "
   (*b*) " Can any gentleman present oblige me with a match ? "

But note also :
   (*c*) He asked me if I had ever seen such a thing in my life.
   (*d*) The old rascal asked if any gentleman present could oblige him with a match.

Other Stops.

(*a*) The mark of exclamation (!)

> Saints alive ! here's the Mayor.
> Hooray !   A week to Christmas !

Do not use the mark of exclamation excessively. Some letter-writers put it at the end of any sentence which they think is apt or sarcastic : e.g.

> He asked me to show him my work.   I'll show him !

What is worse is the habit of imitating the third-rate form of poster advertisement with two or even three exclamation marks : e.g.

Lusher's lovely Lemonade ! Going ! Going ! ! Gone ! ! !

(*b*) Brackets ( ).

Brackets enclose a word, phrase, clause or sentence which may be introduced into the passage by the writer for the purpose of explanation : e.g.

> The ghost (so local rumour has it) walks the moors on moonlight nights between Okehampton and Tavistock.

(*c*) (iii) The dash (—)

There is a hoary story which everyone should know that a professor asked his students what marks of punctuation they would have in the sentence :

> On a bright summer's day a young lady of striking beauty walked briskly down the street.

A young gallant quickly ventured an interesting suggestion : " I should have a dash after the young lady, sir."

The dash is used often too carelessly in English instead of commas.   Its real functions are :

(1) To separate an expression from the rest of the sentence in a similar manner to brackets : e.g.

> The little fellow was spending his time pulling the wool from the garment his mother was making—a rare sport.

(2) After the colon : e.g.

> Dr. Johnson summed up our responsibility admirably as follows :—The future is purchased by the present.

(3) The dash is also used when the sentence is abruptly interrupted and left unconcluded : e.g.

> The Mayoress had now been speaking for over an hour on the privileges and responsibilities of her sex. " I am quite sure," she declared, " that women are, generally speaking—"
>
> " Hear, hear ! " came from the back of the hall.

(4) The dash can also be used in other circumstances, e.g. for emphasis by means of an anticipatory pause : e.g.

> (i) He gave me what I most sincerely desired—permission to leave his evil company.
>
> (ii) We're foot—slog—slog—sloggin' over Africa—
> Foot—foot—foot—foot—sloggin' over Africa—
> (Boots—boots—boots—boots—movin' up and down again.)   (Kipling.)

Avoid, however, the Jingle habit of writing. You will remember Dickens' Mr. Jingle. A sample of his writing appears on page 126. Some people write their letters in the " Jingle " style.

Underlining.—Perhaps it should be stated here that the underlining of words (although Queen Victoria, who was told by Disraeli that she was the head of the literary profession, established a royal precedent) is not a desirable feature in writing. There are other ways of securing emphasis than this. The underlined word should be used on such infrequent occasions that, when it is used, it draws urgent attention to the word.

The Apostrophe.—The apostrophe is used :

(*a*) To indicate a letter or letters omitted : e.g.

don't (do not) ; shan't (shall not) ; o'er (over, ; an' I stopped, an' I looked, an' I listened ; 'twas on a Monday mornin'.

(*b*) to indicate the possessive :

boy's name, man's estate (singular) ;
ladies' department, women's clothes (plural).

Quotation Marks are used :

(*a*) To denote a speaker's *actual* words : e.g.

(i) And Noah he often said to his wife when he sat down to dine, " I don't care where the water goes if it doesn't get into the wine."—CHESTERTON, " Wine and Water."

(ii) If there is one quotation within another it is advisable to enclose the inner quotation with single points (' ') and the outer quotation with double (" ") :

On a tree by a river a little tom-tit
Sang, " Willow, titwillow, titwillow ! "
And I said to him, " Dicky-bird, why do you sit
Singing ' Willow, titwillow, titwillow ' ? "

(iii) If the sentence of a quotation is broken by *he said* or its equivalent, there is no need for a capital letter when the quotation is continued : e.g.

" When a man says he is willin'," said Mr. Barkis, " it's as much as to say that a man's waitin' for an answer."

(*b*) Quotation marks are also used when reference is made to a title of a book, poem, etc. : e.g.

Many critics are of the opinion that " St. Joan " is not only Shaw's finest work but the greatest play since " Hamlet."

Capital Letters

Reference has already been made to the use of capitals under a different section, but the occasions of their use can be indicated as follows :

(*a*) At the beginning of every sentence.

(*b*) At the beginning of a quotation :

Shakespeare said, " The devil can cite Scripture for his purpose."

(*c*) At the beginning of a line of poetry :

Let schoolmasters puzzle their brain
With grammar, and nonsense, and learning,
Good liquor, I stoutly maintain,
Gives genius a better discerning.
GOLDSMITH, " She Stoops to Conquer."

(*d*) With proper nouns and their adjectives : e.g.

Rome, Roman, Napoleon, Napoleonic, Parliament.

(*e*) Names of the Deity :

Lord God of Hosts, be with us yet.

(*f*) The important words in the title of a book, poem, etc. : e.g. Browning's " Childe Roland."

Rupert Brooke was the author of " Lines Written in the Belief that the Ancient Roman Festival of the Dead was called Ambarvalia."

(*g*) Days of the week, months, special festivals, events : e.g. Sunday, December, Easter.

(*h*) The personal pronoun *I*, but not *me* (unless it refers to the Deity), as " Thou shalt have no other gods before Me."

(*i*) The exclamations, Oh ! Eh ! Ugb ! etc.

(*j*) In personifications :

And Truth severe, by fairy Fiction drest.

Exercise 193.—Read the following passages and satisfy yourself that you can justify each of the marks of punctuation and capital letters that are employed :

1.
Charlotte, having seen his body
Borne before her on a shutter,
Like a well-conducted person
Went on cutting bread and butter.
Oh, Vanities of vanities !
How wayward the decrees of Fate are ;
How very weak the very wise,
How very small the very great are !
W. M. THACKERAY.

2.
Hurrah ! hurrah ! we bring the Jubilee !
Hurrah ! hurrah ! the flag that makes you free !
So we sang the chorus from Atlanta to the sea
As we were marching through Georgia.
H. C. WORK.

3. " Never . . . see . . . a dead postboy, did you ? " inquired Sam. " No," rejoined Bob, " I never did." " No ! " rejoined Sam triumphantly, " Nor never will ; and there's another thing that no man ever see, and that's a dead donkey."—DICKENS.

Exercise 194.—Punctuate the following passages, inserting capitals where necessary :

1. The use of force alone is but temporary it may subdue for a moment but it does not remove the necessity of subduing again and a nation is not governed which is perpetually to be conquered—BURKE.

2. tis the voice of the lobster I heard him declare
you have baked me too brown I must sugar my hair
CARROLL.

3. I have been assured by a very knowing american of my acquaintance in london that a young healthy child well nursed is at a year old a most delicious nourishing and wholesome food whether stewed roasted baked or boiled and I make no doubt that it will equally serve in a fricassee or ragout—SWIFT.

4. What was to be done twas perfectly plain that they could not well hang the man over again what was to be done the man was dead nought could be done nought could be said so my lord tomnoddy went home to bed—R. H. BARHAM.

5. do you spell it with a v or a w inquired the judge that depends upon the taste and fancy of the speller my lord replied sam

6. at godwins they lamb holcroft and coleridge were disputing which was the better man as he was or man as he is to be give me says lamb man as he is not to be this saying was the beginning of a friendship between us which I believe still continues—HAZLITT.

Exercise 195.—Punctuate the following conversation between Andy and the Squire, from " Handy Andy," by Samuel Lover :

Ride into the town and see if theres a letter for me said the squire one day to andy yes sir you know where to go to the town sir but do you know where to go in the town no sir and why dont you ask you stupid thief sure id find out sir did not I often tell you to ask what youre to do when you dont know yes sir and why dont you I dont like to be troublesome sir confound you said the squire though he could not help laughing at andys excuse for remaining in ignorance well continued he go to the post office you know the post office I suppose yes sir where they sell gunpowder youre right for once said the squire for his majestys postmaster was the person who had the privilege of dealing in the aforesaid combustible go then to the post office and ask for a letter for me remember not gunpowder but a letter yes sir said andy who got astride his hack and trotted away to the post office on arriving at the shop of the postmaster for that person carried on a brisk trade in groceries gimlets broadcloth and linen drapery andy presented himself at the counter and said I want a letter sir if you please who do you want it for said the postmaster in a tone which andy considered an agression upon the sacredness of private life so andy thought the coolest contempt he could throw upon the prying impertinence of its postmaster was to repeat his question I want a letter sir if you please and who do you want it for repeated the postmaster whats that to you said andy the postmaster laughing at his simplicity told him he could not tell what letter to give him unless he told him the directions the directions I got was to get a letter here thats the directions who gave you those directions the master and whos your master what concern is that o yours

Revision

1. For what purpose is the full stop used in addition to indicate the end of a sentence ?

2. Name the ways in which one clause may be marked off from another.

3. By what marks of punctuation may a direct quotation be introduced, in addition to quotation marks ?

4. On what occasions is a capital letter used in English ?

5. Punctuate the following passages. (There are three sentences) :

give me what I have or even less and therewith let me live to myself for what remains of life if the gods will that anything remain let me have a generous supply of books and of food stored a year ahead nor let me hang and tremble on the hope of the uncertain hour nay it is enough to ask Jove who gives them and takes them away that he grant life and subsistence a balanced mind I will find for myself—HORACE.

KEY TO EXERCISES

Solutions are given to exercises wherever possible. Where the answer would take the form of a definition or an example, the student should refer to the appropriate section and chapter

If, owing to the nature of an exercise, a number of answers can be given, no reference will be made to the questions in the Key.

Ex. 1.

    1. 2. 4. 6. Sentences.   3. 5. Phrases.

Ex. 3.

  (i) Capitals at : *N*ever ; *A*ll ; *T*he *M*ole.
      Full stops after : full-fed river. held again. bubble.
  (ii) Capitals at : *A* wave ; *I*t was ; *W*ith a yell ; *H*e had ;
      I felt.
      Full stops at : escape. exertion. upon us. meet it.
      round us.

Ex. 4.—Some examples :

Statements.   1. Alice waited. . . .
              2. It was Bill.

Questions.   1. Where's the other ladder ?
              2. Who did that ?

Commands.   1. Fetch it here, lad.
              2. Catch hold of this rope.

Exclamation. 1. Oh ! it's coming down !

Ex. 5.

    1. Statement. 2. Qu. 3. Qu. 4. Qu. 5. Command.
    6. Exclam. 7. Statement. 8. Command. 9. Qu.
    10. Exclam.

Ex. 7a.

Subject only given, the rest of the sentence being
    Predicate.

1. The Cardinal. 2. They. 3. Two nice little boys, rather more than grown. 4. Such a terrible curse. 5. That little Jackdaw.

Ex. 7b.

1. who. 2. what. 3. you. 4. what. 5. your name.

Ex. 7c.

1. (you). 2. (you). 3. (you). 4. (you). 5. (you).

Ex. 7d.

1. you. 2. he. 3. he. 4. she. 5. you.

Ex. 7e.

1. you (Billy Boy). 2. (you). 3. (Thou or you). 4. we. 5. God. 6. (Britannia). 7. you (Daisy, Daisy). 8. Thy dwellings. 9. it. 10. we. 11. those feet. 12. the Minstrel Boy.

Revision

1.

1. Sentence : Statement. 2. Phrase. 3. Sentence : Statement. 4. Phrase. 5. Phrase. 6. Phrase. 7. Sentence : Command. 8. Sentence : Question. 9. Sentence : Exclamation. 10. Sentence : Wish.

2.

	Subject	Predicate
1.	The pier	is near.
2.	I	hear the bells.
3.	(You)	get your weapons ready.
4.	Every bullet	has its billet.
5.	Three	is company and two none in married life.
6.	Anybody	can be good in the country.
7.	He	is prepared to run what dangers !
8.	Brother	has followed brother from sunshine to the sunless land how fast !
9.	(You or Thou)	abide with me.
10.	The clustered spires of Frederick green-walled by the hills of Maryland.	stand up from the meadows rich with corn, clear in the cool September morn.

Ex. 8a.

boots (P.), dynamite (S.), grass (S.), mule (S.), fool (S.), school (S.).

Ex. 8b.

sobs (P.), cries (P.), care (S.), cause (S.), Parson Sly (S.), effect (S.), Lubin (S.), wife (S.).

Ex. 8c.

hour (S.), wenches (P.), design (S.), stone (S.), window (S.), stairs (P.), evening (S.), thieves (P.), looking (S.), company (S.), thoughts (P.), fears (P.), fears (P.), men (P.), money (S.), Jane (S.), dog (S.), lodging (S.), noise (S.).

Ex. 8d.

elephantiaphus (S.), coconuts (P.), nose (S.), elephanti-elephantiaphus (S.), cockroach (S.), water-bug (S.), sink (S.).

Ex. 9.

(a) *Common :* bridge, point, bowers, stall, woman, pan, charcoal, feet, hand, arch, scene, bank, river, masts, eye, wharves, edifices, masts, buildings, wreaths, smoke, canopy, city, breast, river, whirlpool, bulwarks, arch, pool.

Proper : Caesar's Castle, White Tower, Needle, Thames, Maelström.

Collective : forest, maze.

Abstract : amazement, superabundance, horror.

(b) statement, yesterday, Mr. A. B. Smith, defective, Force, Mr. Smith, detective, Farce.

Ex. 10.

1. men. 2. tears. 3. peace. 4. loch.

Ex. 11.

flock, herd, pack, covey, swarm, pride, gaggle, litter, school, staff, choir, orchestra, gang (or team), suite, library, range, shrubbery.

Ex. 12.

(a) monkeys, ponies, women, cod, libraries, sheaves, contraltos, marches, waltzes, folios, mottoes, roofs/rooves, memorandums/a, onlookers, lookers-on, ringseats, the Misses Robinson.

(b) 1. A man's friend.   2. A boy's best friend.   3. The lions' den.   4. Thieves' honour.   5. Men's achievements.   6. Women's clothes.   7. A fox's tail.   8. The cook's biscuits.

(c) For the sake of euphony.

Ex. 13.

sow, doe, filly, vixen, hind, goose, duck, nun, spinster, witch, countess, poetess, lady, lady, chauffeuse, widow, policewoman, signora, student, alien.

Ex. 14.

(There will be alternatives to these appended.)

(a) success, adversity; weariness, energy; vigour, weakness; kindness, meanness; tenderness, roughness; bravery, fear; satisfaction, discontent; dullness, interest; concord, discord; condolence, callousness.

(b) 1. principal.   2. cast.   3. cord.   4. allusions.   5. patrolled.   6. serial.   7. biographies.   8. suit.   9. surplice.   10. mails.

Revision

1.

Subject	Predicate
1. The next train	has gone ten minutes ago.
2. (You)	feed the brute.
3. What	is better than presence of mind in a railway accident?
4. (You)	let loose the gorgonzola.
5. I	can actually write my name in the dust on the table.
6. You	must be well-educated.
7. Adam	had 'em.

2.

(a) men (Common), Gotham (Proper), sea (Common), bowl (Common), bowl (Common), song (Common).

(b) fellow (Common), Trinity (Proper), doctor (Common), Divinity (Proper), free-thinking (Abstract), drinking (Abstract), vicinity (Common).

(c) man (Common), Devizes (Proper), ears (Common), sizes (Abstract), one (Common), use (Abstract), prizes (Common).

(*d*) swarm (Collective), bees (Common), May (Proper), load (Common), hay (Common).

(*e*) crowd (Collective).

(*f*) Fred (Proper), father (Common), brother (Common), sister (Common), generation (Collective), nation (Common *or* Collective), Fred (Proper).

Ex. 15.

glide, glow, are, open, close, greet, beckon, lift, present, rises, sees, has, is beholding, pours, is touched, steams, disperses.

Ex. 17.

When used as nouns, the accent is on the first syllable; when used as verbs, accent is on second syllable.

Ex. 18.

donkey, lion, elephant, sheep, cattle, dog (fox), cock, frog, hyena, snake, rook.

Ex. 19.

glide (I.), glow (I.), are (I.), open (T.), close (T.), greet (I.), beckon (I.), lift (T.), present (T.), rises (I.), sees (T.), has (T.), is beholding (T.).

Ex. 21.

1. old.   2. twenty-one.   3. friendly.   4. traitors. 5. experts.   6. choice.

Ex. 22a.

1. blows.   2. settle.   3. know.   4. moves.   5. goes. 6. was.

Ex. 22b.

1. is.   2. is.   3. was.   4. was.   5. are.   6. gives. 7. is.   8. was.   9. were.   10. was.

Ex. 23.

1. Present Simple.   2. Historic Present.   3. Present Simple for a general truth.   4. Present Simple for a general truth.   5. Present Simple to introduce quotation.   6. Present Simple to express Future.   7. Present Continuous.   8. Present Continuous expressing future.   9. Present Perfect.   10. Present Perfect.

Ex. 24.

had questioned (Past Perf.) . . . had seen (Past Perf.)
She had said (Past Perf.) there were (Past Simple) . . .
had gone forward (Past Perf.), she had escaped (Past
Perf.). In the yard he had stopped (Past Perf.) . . .
had shut (Past Perf.), had taken (Past Perf.) and had
asked (Past Perf.) . . . One had acknowledged (Past
Perf.) . . . had been told (Past Perf.) . . . owned (Past
Simple) . . . had found (Past Perf.).

Ex. 25.

1. Future.   2. Necessity.   3. Promise.   4. Promise.
5. Future.   6. Determination.   7. Bequest.   8. Wish.

Ex. 26.

had been boasting (Past Perf. Cont.), had hunted (Past
Perf.), am telling (Pres. Cont.), have seen (Pres. Perf.),
declared (Past Simple), shall return (Fut. Simple),
long (Pres. Simple), asked (Past Simple), had visited
(Past Perf.), replied (Past Simple), visited (Past
Simple), shall be staying (Fut. Cont.), remember
(Pres. Simple), happened (Past Simple), asked (Past
Simple), will tell (Fut. Simple), answered (Past
Simple), beamed (Past Simple), had gone (Past Perf.),
had promised (Past Perf.), would allow (Future in the
past), was making (Past Cont.), made (Past Simple),
drawled (Past Simple), was (Past Simple), found (Past
Simple), burst (Past Simple), are laughing (Pres.
Cont.), demanded (Past Simple), am telling (Pres.
Cont.), could speak (Past Simple).

Ex. 27.

1. were angered (townsfolk).   2. is supported (Mayor).
3. will be opposed (they).   4. have been informed (you).
5. is being canvassed (the town).

Ex. 28.

1. We were supplied with a first-rate meal by the landlady.   2. The summit was reached first by Tom at
noon.   3. A rest was taken by all of us under the

shade of a boulder. 4. The route home was pointed
out by the guide. 5. In the gathering darkness, Tom
was lost sight of by the rest of the company.

Ex. 29.

1. shall report (A.). 2. was knocked (P.). 3. have
been warned (P.). 4. was trapped (P.). 5. have
been (A.). 6. will be sailing (A.). 7. had finished (A.).
8. was received (P.). 9. was knitted (P.). 10. are
shipped (P.).

Ex. 30.

1. We were shown a short *cut* by the old shepherd.
2. The old rogue was paid five *pounds* for that cycle by
Robin. 3. A reward of ten shillings was offered the
finder by the Police. 4. After that rebuff he was
asked no further *questions* by his enemies. 5. He will
be taught a *lesson* by that.

Ex. 31.

1. besought. 2. hanged. 3. bidden. 4. broadcast.
5. borne. 6. broken. 7. ridden. 8. eaten. 9. laid.
10. trodden.

Ex. 32.

1. S. 2. W. 3. S. 4. W. 5. S. 6. W. 7. S. 8. W.
9. W. 10. W.

Ex. 33.

1. picking (N.), made (F.). 2. seizing (N.), knocked (F.).
3. suspected (N.), hated (N.), retired (F.). 4. holding (N.), settled (F.). 5. snubbed (N.), mocked (N.),
ridiculed (N.), humiliated (N.), had (F.).

Ex. 37.

1. singing (clown). 2. dead (men). 3. dignified (look).
4. toiling, rejoicing, sorrowing (he). 5. crowded (hour).
6. laid (each).

Ex. 38.

1. As we arrived late, the best . . . 2. As it was
Wednesday afternoon . . . 3. While I was standing . . .
4. Shutting the door with a violent bang, he received

a severe protest . . . 5. Hoping to reduce his temperature, the doctor . . . 6. As they regarded him as . . .

Ex. 40.

1. to run, to chase. 2. to mend. 3. to see. 4. to
bury, to praise. 5. enter. 6. bind. 7. understand.
8. to sit, see, toil. 9. speak. 10. go. 11. to have
taken. 12. have forgotten. 13. about to be married.
14. have helped.

Revision

2. (a) would thrive ; must rise ; hath thriven ; may lie.
(b) married (Obj. wife), is, wish. (c) killed (Obj. Cock
Robin).

3. (a) draw (Imp.), sit (Imp.), spin (Imp.), take (Imp.),
    drink (Imp.), call (Imp.).
(b) is (Indic.), sees (Indic.), hears (Indic.), do (Indic.), am
    (Indic.).
(c) may grow (Subj.).
(d) must gie (Indic.), gie (Indic.).
(e) Let loose (Imp.).
(f) implore (Indic.), to go (Infin.), sin (Infin.), be (Subj.),
    to go (Infin.).

4. (a) *hanged*, past participle of weak, transitive verb " to
    hang," qualifying noun " Harrison."
    looking, present participle of weak, intransitive verb
    " to look," qualifying pronoun " he."
    do. Infinitive of weak verb " to do," forming with
    auxiliary " could " the finite verb " could do." Used
    intransitively.
(b) *Hanging*. Verbal noun forming subject of verb *is*.
(c) *fishing*. Gerund formed from verb " to fish."
(d) *do*. (i) Auxiliary verb, part of finite verb " do do,"
    verb to subject " you."
    do (ii) Infinitive following auxiliary " do." Intransi-
    tively used.
(e) *shall do*. Verb, 1st person plural. Active Voice.
    Transitively used, from weak verb " to do."

5. (*a*) *are*. Present Simple, Active. *am feeling*. Present Continuous, Active.

(*b*) *will be*. Future Simple, Active.

(*c*) *was falling*. Past Continuous, Active.
were crying, were calling. Past Continuous, Active.

(*d*) *hast been called*. Present Perfect, Passive.
is. Present Simple, Active.
have called. Present Perfect, Active.

(*e*) *has saved*. Present Perfect, Active.

(*f*) *have quarrelled*. Present Perfect, Active.
has quarrelled. Present Perfect, Active.
is absolved. Present Simple, Passive.

Ex. 42.

(Only suggestion.) (*a*) wise judge, patient nurse, skilful doctor, eloquent preacher, smart soldier, cunning fox, timid sheep, obstinate mule, faithful dog, busy bee, heavy shower, high wind.

(*b*) Obliging, exorbitant, rough, imminent, simple, guilty.

Ex. 44.

Dutch, Norwegian, Spanish, Swiss, Swedish, Cuban, Peruvian, Parisian, Athenian, Neapolitan, Viennese, Aberdonian.

Ex. 45.

(i) (*a*) eventful, joyous(ful), homely, talkative, momentous(ary), modish, moody, demoniacal, serpentine, burdensome, critical, controllable, realistic, godly.

(*b*) Christian, Confucian, Mahometan, Buddhist, Caesarean, Napoleonic, Hitlerite, Gladstonian, Homeric, Shakespearean, Miltonic, Shavian.

(ii) mannish, manly; womanly, womanish; respectful, respectable; officious, official; luxurious, luxuriant; contemptuous, contemptible; graceful, gracious; creditable, credited; friendly, friendless; brutal, brutish.

(iii) ignorant, bright, costly, innocent, vicious, lazy, eternal, dangerous, friendly, permanent.

Ex. 46.

1. many.   2. few.   3. several.   4. innumerable.
5. several.   (Others could be suggested.)

Ex. 47.

Some examples: third degree, fourth dimension,
sixth sense, seventh heaven, eighth wonder of the
world, eleventh hour, twelfth man, nineteenth hole,
twenty-first birthday, fiftieth anniversary, hundredth
man.

Ex. 48.

1. fourteen, six.   2. few.   3. few, few, few, enough.
4. little.   5. half, all, other.   6. both, some, little.

Ex. 49.

1. fewer.   2. a poor.   3. a.   4. an hotel.   5. many.

Ex. 50.

kinder, kindest; more, most benevolent; more,
most loving; better, best; purer, purest; holier,
holiest; more, most innocent; divine; harder,
hardest; more, most cruel (sometimes: crueller,
cruellest); worse, worst; worse, worst; more, most
wicked; smaller, smallest; less/lesser, least; tinier, tini-
est; later/latter, latest/last; outer/utter (archiac), out-
most/outermost, utmost/uttermost; farther, farthest.

Ex. 51.

1. any other speaker in.   2. stronger than it.   3. omit
others.   4. omit *before*.   5. omit *other*.   6. *better*, not
best.   7. omit *more—to retire*; omit *than*.   8. *greater*,
not *greatest*

Ex. 52.

Suggestions: *their* nests, *sincere* proposal, *attractive*
hen, *her* suitor, *hostile* frame, *loving* male, *shrewish*
hen, *bitter* savagery, *such* behaviour, *persistent*
suitor, *his fond* endearments, *obstinate* hen, *many*
refusals, *his* charms. *What* persistence, completely
submissive, *her* beak, *her* suitor's, *his* feet, *ardent* love.
Love affairs, *other* people, *amusing*. *Our own*, con-
siderable.

Ex. 53.

notorious (Ql.), their (P.), own (Em.), endless (Ql.), each (Di.), much (Qn.), these (D.), cock (Ql.), great (Ql.), many (Qn.), neighbouring (Ql.), his (P.), more (Qn.), another (Qn.), rascally (Ql.), few (Qn.), uninterested (Ql.), nearest (Ql.), what (In.), her (P.), own (Em.), her (P.), very (Em.), cock (Ql.), his (P.), recent (Ql.), bur-glarious (Ql.), another (Qn.).

Ex. 54.

1. principal. 2. dual. 3. stationary. 4. that. 5. mis-cellaneous. 6. this.

Ex. 58.

1. in chains. 2. at the corner. 3. in the distance. 4. with promise. 5. of high power.

Ex. 59.

1. the hill-top. 2. flaxen-haired, hatless, ginger-haired. 3. uncontrollable. 4. punctual. 5. apt.

Ex. 60.

1. exempt. 2. gullible. 3. ambidextrous. 4. sub-marine. 5. irascible. 6. inimitable. 7. irreparable. 8. unanimous. 9. credulous. 10. initial.

Ex. 62.

1. ambiguous. 2. inappropriate. 3. inexcusable. 4. inescapable. 5. ill-tempered, choleric.

Revision

2. (i) parent (Common), numbers (Common), duty (Ab-stract), fault (Common), boon (Common), matter (Common), pleasure (Abstract), force (Abstract).

(ii) two (Quantity), warm (Quality), cold (Quality), law-ful (Quality), unlawful (Quality), good (Quality), extraordinary (Quality).

(iii) I am just two and two. I am warm.

	Subject	Predicate
(iv)	I	am just two and two
	I	am warm

(v) *taken*. past participle of verb " to take " (weak, transitive verb), qualifying noun " matter."

Ex. 64.

1. me. 2. he. 3. she. 4. we. 5. me. 6. they.
7. me. 8. he.

Ex. 65.

1. The manager, who had been ruined, told his friend.
2. Whenever the Sealyham met the little Cairn, the
larger dog wagged . . . 3. She quarrelled regularly
with her sister, who . . . 4. in his *own* hands. 5. The
vicar complimented the curate on being an excellent . . .

Ex. 66.

1. You and John . . . 2. You and she . . . 3. You
and the Jacksons . . . 4. We and Mr. and Mrs.
Holroyd . . . 5. You and the children . . . 6. He
and I . . . 7. I, sir. 8. *are*. 9. *am*. 10. *is*.

Ex. 67.

1. it's. 2. yours. 3. women's, hers. 4. there's.
5. theirs.

Ex. 68.

1. this. 2. that. 3. that, this. 4. these, those.
5. this, that.

Ex. 69.

1. who. 2. what. 3. what. 4. which. 5. who.
6. whom. 7. whom. 8. who.

Ex. 70.

1. goes. 2. does. 3. makes. 4. is.

Ex. 71.

1. myself (Em.). 2. himself (Em.). 3. herself (Refl.).
4. yourself (Em.). 5. themselves (Refl.). 6. yourself (Em.). 7. yourself (Refl.).

Ex. 72.

we (P.), one (I.), he (P.), himself (Em.), we (P.),
him (P.), he (P.), each (D.), us (P.), him (P.), this (Dem.),
we (P.), it (P.), ours (P.), we (P.), we (P.), that (Dem.),
somebody (In.), we (P.), we (P.), other (In.), we (P.),
ourselves (Refl.), anyone (In.), us (P.).

Ex. 73.

1. It was an even game, *which* was watched by a crowd of spectators (game—Nom.).   2. The home team, *who* had the advantage of the presence of their own supporters, wore white (team—Nom.).   3. The visiting side, *who* had travelled overnight from the North, wore colours (side—Nom.).   4. The referee, *who* was the object of many remarks, not always courteous, from the crowd, was kept very busy (referee—Nom.).   5. The captain of the home team, *whom* the local supporters constantly cheered, was a tower of strength to his side (captain—Acc.).   6. The referee gave a penalty, *which* the right back took, for offside against the home team (penalty—Acc.).

Ex. 74.

1. who. 2. whom. 3. whom. 4. who. 5. whom. 6. who.

Ex. 75.

1. Mrs. Major Robertson, *who* had great beauty, energy, courage and sense, was a woman of slight build.   2. One night she went to her bedroom, *which* was at the top of the house.   3. She left downstairs a young watchman *who* was the only other occupant of the house.   4. Entering her bedroom she saw a portion of a man's foot *which* was projecting from under the bed.   5. She gave no cry of alarm *which* would have disturbed the thief, but she began to undress.   6. Suddenly she stamped her foot, addressing herself aloud in words *which* the burglar could hear.   7. "There, I've forgotten the key, *which* I'm always leaving downstairs."   8. Leaving the candle burning and the door open, she went down to the young watchman, *who* listened to her story and returned to the bedroom with her.   9. The watchman secured the proprietor of the foot, *which* had not moved an inch.   10. How many women are there *who* could show such cool common sense ?

Ex. 76.

1. (that) we rented. 2. (whom) you want. 3. (that) I like best. 4. (whom) you like. 5. (which) the car

made. 6. (whom) I am courting; (that) she had ever seen.

Ex. 79.

1. who (man). 2. which (lane). 3. whom (actor). 4. that (songs). 5. as (man). 6. as (jokes). 7. that (all). 8. where, *rel. adv.* (hotel).

Ex. 81.

c.	Pronoun	Kind	Number	Person	Gender	Case	Reason for Case
1	I She	Pers. Pers.	S. S.	1st 3rd	Fem. Fem.	Nom. Nom.	Subject of verb *go*. Subject of verb *said*.
2	Who	Int.	S.	3rd	Com.	Nom.	Subject of verb *will*.
3	Anyone	Ind.	S.	3rd	Com.	Nom.	Subject of verb *has seen*.
4	That	Dem.	S.	3rd	Neut.	Nom.	Subject of verb *is*.
5	Such Some You	Dem. Ind. Pers.	P. P. P.	3rd 3rd 2nd	Com. Com. Com.	Nom. Nom. Acc.	Subject of verb *were*. Complement of *were*. After preposition *of*.
6	I Which I	Pers. Rel. Pers.	S. S. S.	1st 3rd 1st	Com. Neut. Com.	Nom. Acc. Nom.	Subject of *chose*. Object of preposition *on*. Subject of *had given*.
7	Each	Ind.	S.	3rd	Masc.	Acc.	Object of *let*.
8	He What Hisn He He	Pers. Rel. Poss. Pers. Pers.	S. S. S. S. S.	3rd 3rd 3rd 3rd 3rd	Masc. Masc. Masc. Masc. Masc.	Nom. Nom. Nom. Nom. Nom.	Subject of *prigs*. Subject of *is*. Complement after *is*. Subject of *is copped*. Subject of *will go*.
9	It	Pers.	S.	3rd	Neut.	Acc.	Object of *fetch*.
	Yourself	Emph.	S.	2nd	Com.	Nom.	Agreeing with (you) *fetch*.
10	She Herself	Pers. Reflex.	S. S.	3rd 3rd	Fem. Fem.	Nom. Acc.	Subject of *fancies*. Object of *fancies*.

Revision

2. (i) Jehu.   (ii) Cain.   (iii) Adam and Eve.   (iv) Wise Men from the East.   (v) St. Peter.   (vi) Judas.

3. (i) Personal.   (ii) Personal.   (iii) Personal.   (iv) Personal.   (v) Personal.   (vi) Personal.

5. (i) Pronoun.   (ii) Adjective, adjective.   (iii) Adjective, adjective.   (iv) Adjective, pronoun.   (v) Pronoun, adjective, adjective, pronoun.   (vi) Pronoun, pronoun, pronoun, pronoun, pronoun.

Ex. 87.

solemnly (M.), outside the booking office (P.), in heavy black (M.), in his hand (P.), then (T.), as he advanced (T.), instantly (T.), equally (M.), to Perth (P.), in a gloomy voice (M.), as he handed his wreath to his neighbour (T.), whilst his hand went to his pocket (T.), after he had peered through the window at the dour faces (T.).

Ex. 88.

1. You will see with half an eye that . . . 2. The organist played a voluntary with much feeling whilst the rector . . . 3. When the speaker sat down, the audience . . . 4. Generally speaking, ladies are . . . 5. In my view, he should . . .

Ex. 91.

1. Sentence-word. 2. Sentence-word. 3. Sentence-word. 4. Adverb of affirmation. 5. Adjective of quantity. 6. Adverb of degree. 7. Noun. 8. Sentence-word. 9. Sentence-word. 10. Noun.

Ex. 92.

(a) smoothly, moodily, dramatically, callously, majestically, gaily, well, fast.

(b) momentarily, hourly, daily, asleep, lengthwise, betimes, heavenwards, besides, ashore.

Ex. 93.

(i) *homely, slovenly, sickly,* etc. (ii) Use an adverbial phrase : *in a homely way.* (iii) e.g. *agile, wily,* etc., where the normal adverb formation would be un-euphonious.

Ex. 94.

1. Adj. 2. Adv. 3. Adj. 4. Adv. 5. Adj. 6. Adv. 7. Adj. 8. Adv. 9. Adj. 10. Adj. 11. Adj. 12. Adv.

Ex. 95.

sooner, more tenderly, more, latter, oftener, nearer, worse, further, faster.

G

Ex. 97.

1. fluently. 2. reluctantly. 3. carelessly. 4. intermittently. 5. seldom. 6. humbly.

Ex. 99.

(a) 1. too (Degree, *many*). 2. never (Time, *rains*). 3. best (Manner, Super., *laughs*) ; last (Time, Super., *laughs*). 4. well (Manner, Pos., *begun*) ; half (Manner, *done*). 5. once (Time, *bitten*) ; twice (Time, [*are*] *shy*). 6. soonest (Time, Super., *mended*) ; (b) down (Place, *dropt*) ; down (Place, *dropt*) ; only (Degree, *break*) ; (c) long (Manner, Pos., *lives*) ; well (Manner, Pos., *lives*).

Revision

2. (i) weary, unfortunate, young, fair.
   (ii) tenderly, slenderly ; rashly, so.
   (iii) weary of breath.
   (iv) to her death ; with care.

3. *Subject.*   *Predicate*
   (You)   take her up tenderly
   (You)   lift her with care, fashioned so tenderly,
              young and so fair.

Ex. 101.

1. on. 2. down. 3. in/of. 4. upon, in. 5. beyond.

Ex. 102.

1. on. 2. over. 3. at. 4. behind. 5. against. 6. from/off.

Ex. 103.

Prepositions in italics.

(a) 1. writes *for* a living. 2. is *near* the sea. 3. dilly-dally *by* the way. 4. left *for* a handful. 5. has gone *beyond* recall.

(b) 1. proud *of* his achievement. 2. clever *with* the brush. 3. heavy *with* dew. 4. good *at* what ?

(c) 1. mass *of* ruins. 2. hole *in* the wall. 3. walk *along* the shore. 4 house *with* the garage. 5. nap *after* dinner.

Ex. 104.

1. to (me), with (eyes). 2. o'er (downs), with (me). 3. upon (seat), of (bicycle), for (two). 4. in (Scotland), before (ye). 5. for (whom). 6. from (him). 7. to (me). 8. to (thee). 9. at ('em). 10. to (fair), by (light), of (moon), of (bunk), down (trunk), on (knees), of (monk-ey).

Ex. 105.

1. me. 2. him. 3. me. 4. him. 5. us. 6. whom. 7. her. 8. whom.

Ex. 106.

(a) 1. of. 2. for. 3. of. 4. over. 5. toward. 6. of.

(b) 1. of. 2. to. 3. on. 4. with. 5. to *or* from. 6. with.

(c) 1. from. 2. of. 3. with. 4. from. 5. into. 6. against.

Ex. 107.

1. for. 2. of. 3. with. 4. to. 5. on. 6. over. 7. of. 8. in. 9. in. 10. into. 11. beside. 12. besides. 13. between. 14. among. 15. at, in.

Ex. 108.

1. past. 2. past. 3. past. 4. passed. 5. past. 6. passed.

Ex. 109.

1. Prep. 2. Adv. 3. Adv., Adv. 4. Prep. 5. Adv. 6. Prep. 7. Prep. 8. Adv. 9. Prep. 10. Adv.

Ex. 110.

Adv., Adv., Prep., Adv.

Ex. 111.

1. *with what* to *to what*. 2. *between* to *among*. 3. *to me* to *as far as I am concerned*, or omit. 4. *he* to *him*. 5. *different to* to *different from*; *like* to *as*. 6. Why do you want to be read to ? 7. Omit *more* ; *than* to *to*.

Revision

2. (a) (i) for, among, into, in ; (ii) of, in, betwixt.
   (b) (iii) Alas ! (iv) Ugh !

3. different *from*, prefer *to*, contact *with*, expert *in*, hostile *to*, dealer *in*, accessory *to*.

G*

Ex. 112.

   1. Words, words, sentences, sentences.
   2. Sentences, sentences, words.
   3. Words.   4. Words.   **5.** Sentences.
   6. Clauses on each occasion.

Ex. 114.

   1. and. 2. but. 3. though. 4. or. **5.** until. 6. before.
   7. while. 8. that.

Ex. 116.

   1. Conj. **2.** Prep. **3.** Prep. 4. Conj. **5.** Prep.
   6. Conj.

Ex. 117.

   1. Delight. 2. Annoyance. **3.** Contempt. **4.** Disgust.
   5. Disapproval. 6. Caution.

Ex. 118.

   1. Bible. **2.** Shakespeare. **3.** Scotland. 4. Wales.
   5. Germany. 6. America. 7. Spain. 8. France.
   9. Ireland. **10.** North England.

Revision

   1. (*a*) Multiplication (Nominative), Vexation (Nominative), Division (Nominative), Rule (Nominative), Practice (Nominative).

     (*b*) *as* (Conjunction), *of* (Preposition), *doth* (Auxiliary verb), *and* (Conjunction).

   2. (*a*)   *Subject*   *Predicate.*
     Three wise men of Gotham   went to sea in a bowl.

     (*b*) *Three.* Adjective, Quantity, Numeral, qualifying noun *men*.
     my. Adjective, Possessive, qualifying noun *song*.
     longer. Adjective, Quality, Comparative degree, Predicatively used, qualifying noun *song*.

   3. (*a*) *Conjunctions :* as, and.
     Prepositions : to, with, to.

(*b*) *was going*. Verb, Intransitive, Weak, Active, 1st Person Singular, Past Continuous, forming predicate to pronoun *I*.

every. Adjective, Distributive, qualifying noun *wife*.

Ex. 124 (briefly given).

1. Subjunctive mood, expressing wish. 2. Verbal noun. 3. Nominative absolute. 4. Retained object. 5. Cognate object. 6. Exclamatory pronoun. 7. Adverb. 8. Accusative case governed by *of*. 9. Genitive for " at Selfridge's Store." 10. Gerund. 11. Emphasising pronoun. 12. Relative pronoun. 13. Relative pronoun to express negative. 14. Cognate object. 15. Indirect object. 16. Adjective with passive meaning. 17. Imperative mood, or may be regarded as preposition. 18. Subjunctive mood. 19. Simple Present Tense to indicate future. 20. Present participle. 21. Predicative noun. 22. Adverb of degree. 23. Emphasising adjective. 24. Adverb. 25. Adjective used as adverb. 26. Vocative case.

Ex. 125.

1. *unless* to *except*. 2. Everyone of us has to bring his lunch and tea with him. 3. to quarrel constantly with honest folk like you and me. 4. I am pleased to accept. 5. *latter* to *last*. 6. *the factory, etc.* to *would make the factory a happier place*. 7. *lain* to *laid*, *me* to *my*. 8. *her* to *the* sisters; *most well spoken* to *best spoken*. 9. *but feel* to *feeling*. 10. *I* to *me*, *he* to *him*. 11. *or* to *and*. 12. *will* to *shall*. 13. *all others* to *any*. 14. *were* to *was*. 15. *exalt* to *exult*. 16. As they were co-directors, the issue . . . among the three men. 17. *Who* to *whom*, omit *most*. 18. It was he at whom (at him that) the blow was aimed. 19. Mixed metaphor. 20. *complements* to *compliments*; *I shall* to *he will*; *I have* to *he has*. 21. omit *vacant*. 22. taken to the Northbridge Hospital in an unconscious condition where . . . 23. He comes to see me only when he wants to borrow something from me. 24. centres *in*. 25. While I was walking. 26. one's own home.

27. *whom* to *who*.   28. Is either of these girls more accurate at her work than I ?   29. Nobody but you and me need know the real circumstances that led to his dismissal.   30. *Whom* to *who*.

Revision

3. (i) *me*. Popular use of the accusative case after verb " to be," where nominative would technically be more correct. Cf. French *C'est moi*.

 (ii) *but* is usually regarded as a preposition and is followed by accusative case. Here it must be regarded as a conjunction in the sense, " but only Thou fightest for us."

(iii) *than* is usually regarded as a conjunction and the nominative *who* might be expected. By using an accusative *whom*, Milton is regarding *than* as a preposition.

(iv) *Whom* is the incorrect case. The nominative case should be used as being the complement to the verb " to be " : " Who (say men that) am I ? "

 (v) *my*. Possessive adjective, qualifying noun equivalent " going." Correctly used.

Ex. 126.

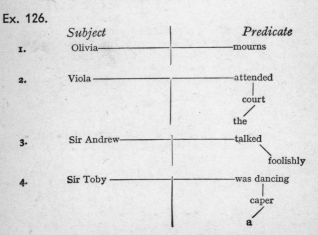

	Subject	*Predicate*
1.	Olivia	mourns
2.	Viola	attended court the
3.	Sir Andrew	talked foolishly
4.	Sir Toby	was dancing caper a

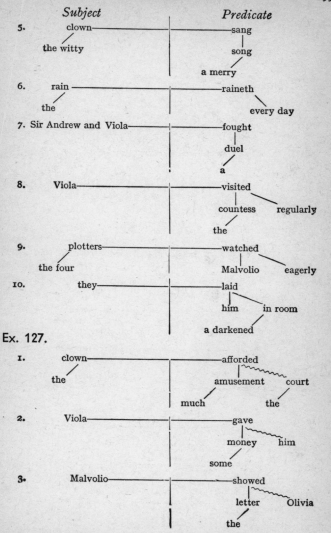

Subject | *Predicate*

5. clown————————sang
   the witty
   song
   a merry

6. rain ————————raineth
   the
   every day

7. Sir Andrew and Viola————fought
   duel
   a

8. Viola————————visited
   countess   regularly
   the

9. plotters————————watched
   the four
   Malvolio   eagerly

10. they————————laid
    him   in room
    a darkened

Ex. 127.

1. clown————————afforded
   the
   amusement   court
   much   the

2. Viola————————gave
   money   him
   some

3. Malvolio————————showed
   letter   Olivia
   the

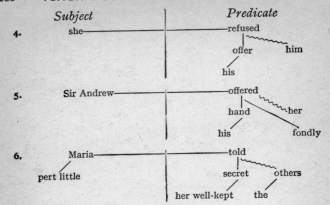

Subject		*Predicate*

4.   she————refused
          offer   him
          his

5.   Sir Andrew————offered
               hand   her
               his   fondly

6.   Maria————told
    pert little   secret   others
          her well-kept   the

Ex. 130.

1. Comp. 2. Obj. 3. Adv. 4. Obj. 5. Comp. 6. Adv.
7. Obj. 8. Adv. 9. Comp. 10. Obj. 11. Adv.
12. Adv. 13. Obj. 14. Comp. 15. Comp. 16. Adv.

Ex. 131.

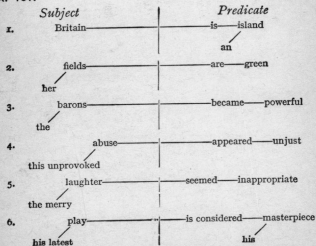

Subject		*Predicate*

1.   Britain————is————island
                     an

2.   fields————are————green
    her

3.   barons————became————powerful
    the

4.   abuse————appeared————unjust
    this unprovoked

5.   laughter————seemed————inappropriate
    the merry

6.   play————is considered————masterpiece
    his latest   his

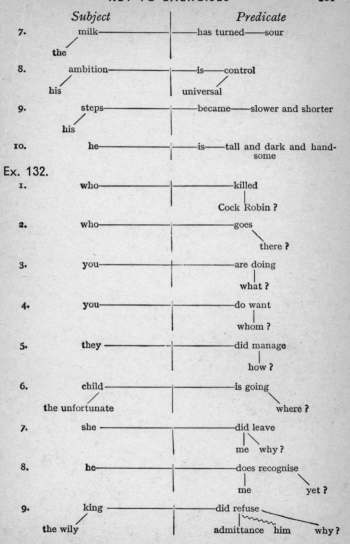

	Subject		*Predicate*

7. milk — has turned — sour
   the

8. ambition — is — control
   his   universal

9. steps — became — slower and shorter
   his

10. he — is — tall and dark and handsome

Ex. 132.

1. who — killed
      Cock Robin ?

2. who — goes
      there ?

3. you — are doing
      what ?

4. you — do want
      whom ?

5. they — did manage
      how ?

6. child — is going
   the unfortunate   where ?

7. she — did leave
      me   why ?

8. he — does recognise
      me   yet ?

9. king — did refuse
   the wily   admittance   him   why ?

	Subject		*Predicate*

10.   farmer ——————————————————— will offer

  the old   what ? him   probably
                                                                    tomorrow

Ex. 133.

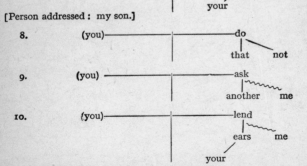

1.   (you) ————————————— halt

2.   (you) ————————————— look

             yonder

3.   (you) ————————————— mind

             heads

         your

4.   (you) ————————————— be ——— quiet

5.   (you) ————————————— give

             hand   me

         your

6.   (you) ————————————— appear ——— unmoved

7.   (you) ————————————— give

             heart   me

         your

[Person addressed : my son.]

8.   (you) ————————————— do

             that   not

9.   (you) ————————————— ask

             another   me

10.   (you) ————————————— lend

             ears   me

         your

[Persons addressed : Friends, Romans, Countrymen.]

Ex. 134.

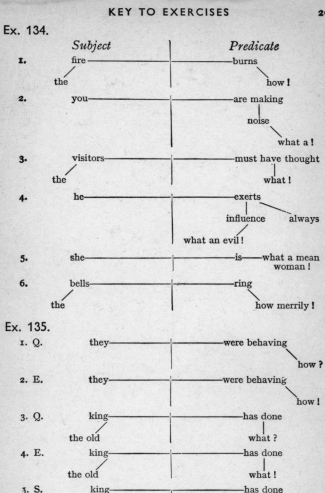

	Subject	*Predicate*
1.	fire — the	burns — how !
2.	you —	are making — noise — what a !
3.	visitors — the	must have thought — what !
4.	he —	exerts — influence — always — what an evil !
5.	she —	is — what a mean woman !
6.	bells — the	ring — how merrily !

Ex. 135.

1. Q.	they —	were behaving — how ?
2. E.	they —	were behaving — how !
3. Q.	king — the old	has done — what ?
4. E.	king — the old	has done — what !
5. S.	king — the old	has done — work — a noble

[My word : Exclamation phrase.]

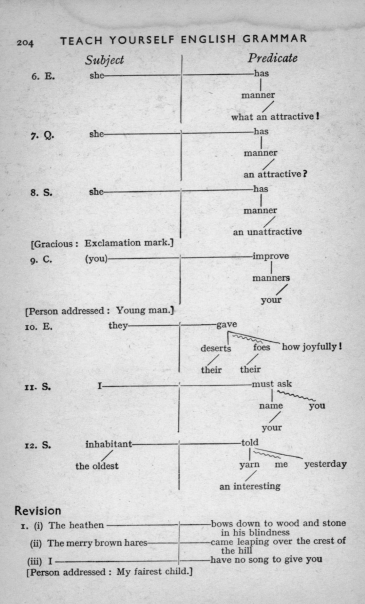

Subject | *Predicate*

6. E. she———————has
manner
what an attractive !

7. Q. she———————has
manner
an attractive ?

8. S. she———————has
manner
an unattractive

[Gracious : Exclamation mark.]

9. C. (you)———————improve
manners
your

[Person addressed : Young man.]

10. E. they————gave
deserts foes how joyfully !
their their

11. S. I————must ask
name you
your

12. S. inhabitant————told
the oldest yarn me yesterday
an interesting

Revision

1. (i) The heathen————bows down to wood and stone in his blindness

(ii) The merry brown hares————came leaping over the crest of the hill

(iii) I————have no song to give you

[Person addressed : My fairest child.]

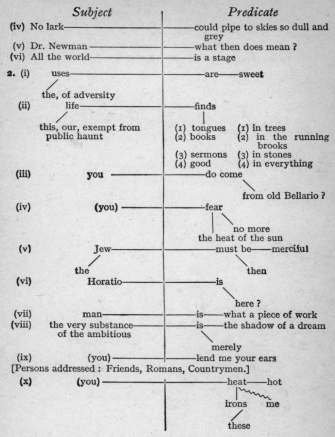

	Subject	Predicate

(iv) No lark——could pipe to skies so dull and grey

(v) Dr. Newman——what then does mean ?

(vi) All the world——is a stage

2. (i) uses——are——sweet
the, of adversity

(ii) life——finds
this, our, exempt from public haunt
(1) tongues (1) in trees
(2) books (2) in the running brooks
(3) sermons (3) in stones
(4) good (4) in everything

(iii) you——do come
from old Bellario ?

(iv) (you)——fear
no more
the heat of the sun

(v) Jew——must be——merciful
the then

(vi) Horatio——is
here ?

(vii) man——is——what a piece of work

(viii) the very substance of the ambitious——is——the shadow of a dream
merely

(ix) (you)——lend me your ears
[Persons addressed : Friends, Romans, Countrymen.]

(x) (you)——heat——hot
irons me
these

3. (i) *adversity*. Accusative, governed by preposition " of."

(ii) *Sermons*. Accusative. Object of verb " finds."

(iii) *you*. Nominative. Subject of verb " do come."

(iv) *heat*. Accusative. Object of verb " fear."

(vii) *piece*. Nominative. Complement of verb " is."

(viii) *shadow.* Nominative. Complement of verb " is."

(ix) *me.* Indirect Object.

(x) *me.* Indirect Object, sometimes in this use referred to as the Ethic Dative (e.g. " for my advantage ").

Ex. 136.

1. an old sailor. 2. the Mayor-elect. 3. my favourite author. 4. overlooking the Broads. 5. a man of herculean strength.

Ex. 137.

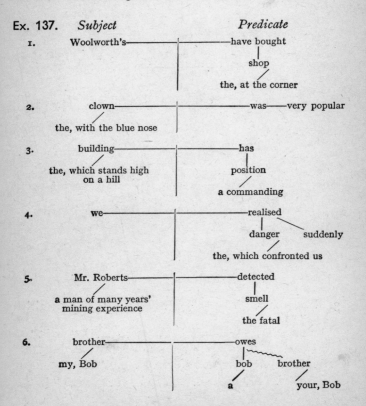

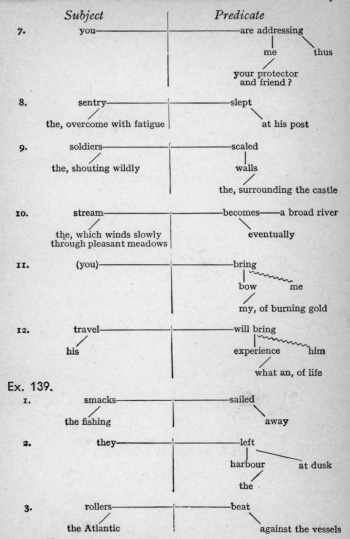

Subject | *Predicate*

7. you——are addressing
             me   thus
          your protector
          and friend ?

8. sentry——slept
    the, overcome with fatigue   at his post

9. soldiers——scaled
    the, shouting wildly   walls
        the, surrounding the castle

10. stream——becomes——a broad river
    the, which winds slowly   eventually
    through pleasant meadows

11. (you)——bring
        bow   me
        my, of burning gold

12. travel——will bring
    his   experience   him
        what an, of life

Ex. 139.

1. smacks——sailed
    the fishing   away

2. they——left
        harbour   at dusk
        the

3. rollers——beat
    the Atlantic   against the vessels

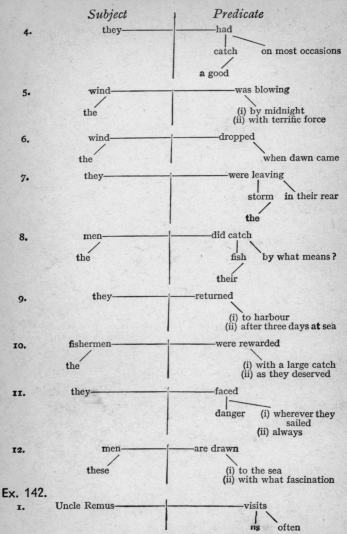

Subject	Predicate

4. they ———— had
     catch   on most occasions
     a good

5. wind ———— was blowing
   the   (i) by midnight
           (ii) with terrific force

6. wind ———— dropped
   the   when dawn came

7. they ———— were leaving
           storm   in their rear
           the

8. men ———— did catch
   the   fish   by what means?
           their

9. they ———— returned
           (i) to harbour
           (ii) after three days at sea

10. fishermen ———— were rewarded
    the   (i) with a large catch
            (ii) as they deserved

11. they ———— faced
           danger   (i) wherever they
                         sailed
                     (ii) always

12. men ———— are drawn
    these   (i) to the sea
            (ii) with what fascination

Ex. 142.

1. Uncle Remus ———— visits
                     ns   often

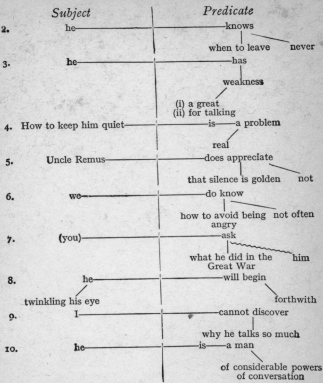

Subject | Predicate

2. he——knows
   when to leave   never

3. he——has
   weakness
   (i) a great
   (ii) for talking

4. How to keep him quiet——is——a problem
   real

5. Uncle Remus——does appreciate
   that silence is golden   not

6. we——do know
   how to avoid being not often
   angry

7. (you)——ask
   what he did in the   him
   Great War

8. he——will begin
   twinkling his eye   forthwith

9. I——cannot discover
   why he talks so much

10. he——is——a man
    of considerable powers
    of conversation

2. (i) intellectual, little.
   (ii) every (boy).
   (iii) that would astonish you.
        That's born into the world alive.
   (iv) often.
   (v) into the world.

Ex. 143.
   (b) in (the) hand, in hand, out of hand, from hand to hand, from hand to mouth, my hands, on hand, on all hands, by hand, at hand, etc.

Ex. 145.

the mice will play ; don't count your chickens ; make hay ; wear it ; all is not gold ; it's a long lane ; he laughs best ; there is always a fire ; speech is silver ; reap a deed.

Ex. 148.

1. No smoking is allowed in the lift. 2. Let the passengers off the car first. 3. There is plenty of room on top. 4. Put your hands up. 5. The more there are, the merrier we shall be. 6. Show tickets, please. 7. The price of petrol is up again. 8. What are you going to do about it ? 9. Go slow. 10. You are a coward !

Ex. 149.

Suggested links : **1**. and. 2. but. 3. *nor* iron bars a cage. 4. and. 5. and, but. 6. and, but. 7. No man can serve two masters ; either he will hate the one and serve the other, or he will serve the one and hate the other.

Ex. 150.

1. D. 2. D. 3. S. 4. S. 5. D. 6. M. 7. D. 8. S. 9. M. 10. S.

Ex. 151.

Suggested renderings :

1. A thunderstorm spoilt the picnic. 2. Owing to the terrific heat, no serious tennis could be played. 3. Darkness overtook the hunt. 4. All his schemes, however ingenious, failed. 5. I was too astonished to speak. 6. She was a beautiful girl, admired by many. 7. Owing to Peggy's illness the holiday had to be postponed. 8. His unconventional dress caused amusement among the villagers. 9. Owing to the roar of the aeroplanes, we could not hear ourselves speak. 10. Although three goals down at half-time, to everyone's surprise we won the match.

Ex. 152.

Main	*Subordinate Adjectival*
1. There was once a man	who fell asleep during a sermon
2. He had a dream	which was most terrifying in character

Main	*Subordinate Adjectival*
3. He was being led to the gallows by a masked man	who was going to hang him
4. The hangman proceeded with his duty	whom he asked to spare him
5. At this point the man's wife tapped him on the neck	who was ashamed to see her husband asleep in church
6. The good woman had done the worst possible thing	whose intention was to awaken her husband
7. Her husband died of shock	who in his dream was awaiting execution
8. A friend of mine saw in it a flaw	(1) who heard this story (2) which you ought also to see

Ex. 153.

1. Give to me the life	(that) I love
2. He repeated the news	(that) he had just heard
3. The story was not appreciated in that company	(that) you told
4. Gibraltar was the next port	at (which) we called
5. The book deals with the French Revolution	(that) I am reading
6. The good outweighs the evil influence	(1) (that) he does (2) (that) his brother exerts

Ex. 154.

1. Co. 2. Sub. 3. Sub. 4. Sub. 5. Co. 6. Sub.
7. Co. 8. Co.

Ex. 155.

1. He was given by the doctor some medicine that was distinctly unpleasant to the mouth. 2. They listened to a sermon that was long, disjointed, but with some good points from an old parson. 3. At Moreton the coach made a stop, which lasted for about ten minutes, for petrol. 4. There was for sale, the property of an old man, a suite of furniture that was well-upholstered and well-sprung. 5. The Management may refuse permission as it considers proper to anyone. 6. A gentleman has lost an umbrella that has a bone handle and steel ribs.

Ex. 156.

1. I have just read Tolstoy's " War and Peace," a book which deals ... and which is thought ... 2. Omit *and*. 3. I was treated with kindness which was beyond all description, and which ... 4. Mr. Newly-rich bought a house which was over three hundred years of age and which he ... 5. Omit *and*.

Ex. 157.

1. as they had done on a previous occasion (correct). 2. as I have never heard before (correct). 3. as I was examined for my Army test (correct to *by whom*). 4. as I did last year (correct to *to which I went last year*). 5. as he was yesterday (correct to *in which he was yesterday*).

Ex. 158.

1. after our guests had gone. 2. before we had set off. 3. when the cat's away. 4. since Joshua kicked him downstairs. 5. while you sleep. 6. ere I go. 7. as long as Mrs. Tittle-Tattle is alive. 8. till we meet. 9. as soon as the alarm was sounded. 10. until you came.

Ex. 159.

1. Adverbial. 2. Adjectival. 3. Adjectival. 4. Adverbial. 5. Adverbial. 6. Adjectival.

Ex. 160.

1. where you leave him. 2. wherever you go. 3. where'er you walk. 4. whither I go. 5. where in days gone by Lady Peel had trod.

Ex. 161.

1. Adv. 2. Adj. 3. Adv. 4. Adj. 5. Adj. 6. Adj.

Ex. 162.

1. as she had lived. 2. as we sow. 3. as he did those in the branch office years ago. 4. than he appears to be. 5. than was at first supposed.

Ex. 164.

1. because she puts on airs and graces. 2. since you must know. 3. as it was late. 4. for the petrol was running very low. 5. seeing that you know everyone's business. 6. in that I have betrayed innocent blood.

Ex. 168.

1. it costs a small fortune to keep him. 2. the country folk could not understand her. 3. he could not easily retract. 4. we had to feel our way. 5. brigades from neighbouring towns had to be called. 6. the enemy ships were able to make good their escape.

Ex. 171.

1. if you speak at all. 2. if you had not supplied the fare. 3. unless you stop. 4. providing that you promise never to do it again. 5. on condition that no one else claimed the places. 6. had you come. 7. if I'll be your serving-man.

Ex. 173.

as the only guard was over eighty (Reason, *thought*) ; so that he could become friendly with the keeper (Purpose, *made*) ; that he persuaded the keeper to allow his daughter to marry Blood's "nephew" (Result, *was successful*) ; when the old man came into the Tower with his daughter for the wedding ceremony (Time, *was seized*) ; while one snatched at the crown (Time, *took*) ; since the latter was too long to be carried inconspicuously (Cause, *was sawn*) ; as they were busily engaged in stowing away the booty (Time *came*) ; although they could have overpowered the youth (Concession, *ran*) ; as they were making their way across St. Catherine's Wharf (Time, *were caught*) ; if King Charles had listened to his advisers (Condition, *would have punished*) ; as he deserved (Manner, *did treat*) ; where other enemies of the State had been banished (Place, *did banish*) ; as Blood had been disappointed in his venture (Time, *was given*) ; provided he mended his ways (Condition, *was given*).

Ex. 175.

1. Noun Subj. App. 2. Adj. 3. Noun Subj. App. 4. Adj. 5. Adj. 6. Noun Subj. App.

Ex. 181.

1. that they would travel by train from Cambridge to London (Noun Cl., Obj. to verb *decided*). 3. that it was a drowsy afternoon (Noun Subj. Cl. in App. to *fact*). 4. what happened next (Noun Subj. Cl., Subj. to verb *constitutes*). 5. that the collector was approaching (Noun Cl., Obj. to *heard*). 6. that he had lost his ticket (Noun Cl., Obj. to *discovered*). 7. what he was

going to do to avoid a second payment of fare (Noun Cl., Obj. of verb *asked*).   8. what Wiggins suggested (Noun Subj. Cl., Subj. of *was*).   9. what Wiggins suggested (Noun Cl., Obj. of prep. *by*).   10. that Wiggins should hide under the seat (Noun Cl., Obj. in App. to noun *idea*).   11. that this was the best scheme (Noun Obj. Cl., Obj. of verb *decided*).   12. that it was also a dirty one (Noun Cl., Subj. of verb *was apparent*).   14. what might have been expected (Noun Subj. Cl., Complement to verb *was*).   15. why there were five tickets for four people (Noun Cl., Obj. to verb *asked*).   16. where their friend was hiding (Noun Cl., Obj. to verb *revealed*).   17. that he prefers travelling under the seat (Noun Subj. Cl. in App. to *it*).

Ex. 183.
1. (i) when the holiday was over.   (Adv. Time.)
   (ii) who had enjoyed their cruise.   (Adj.)
   (iii) that it had been a most instructive and healthy month.   (Noun Obj.)

2. (i) lest you forget again.   (Adv. Purpose.)
   (ii) that parcels are despatched to the Head Office.   (Noun Obj.)
   (iii) which are not claimed within three months.   (Adj.)

3. (i) unless you are seeking a quarrel with a man.   (Adv. Condition.)
   (ii) whom you ought to respect.   (Adj.)
   (iii) that you are penniless.   (Noun App. to Subj.)

4. (i) wherever you go.   (Adv. Place.)
   (ii) what other people would regard as unpardonable insults.   (Noun Obj.)
   (iii) who is readier to forgive.   (Subord. Adj. Clause.)

Revision
1. (i) Complex Sentence.   (ii) Elliptical Sentence.
   (iii) Phrase.   (iv) Multiple Sentence.
   (v) Phrase.   (vi) Simple Sentence.

Ex. 184.

No.	Clause	Link	Kind	Function
1. A	Daniel Defoe records an interesting incident		Main Clause	Independent.
a¹	which occurred at his brother's warehouse		Subord. Adj. Clause	Qualifying noun *incident* in A.
a²	who wrote the Journal of the Plague Year		Subord. Adj. Clause	Qualifying noun *Defoe* in A.
			COMPLEX SENTENCE	
2. A	he saw a woman coming out of the warehouse with some high-crowned hats		Main Clause	Independent.
a¹	he was walking in Swan Alley	whilst	Subord. Adv. Clause of Time	Qualifying verb *saw* in A.
			COMPLEX SENTENCE	
3. A	she told him		Main Clause	Independent.
a¹	there were other people inside the warehouse	that	Subord. Noun Clause	Object of verb *told* in A.
			COMPLEX SENTENCE	
4. A	the fact made him so suspicious		Main Clause	Independent.
a¹	many people were leaving the warehouse with hats	that	Subord. Noun Subj. Clause	In apposition to noun *fact* in A.
a²	he went inside	that	Subord. Adv. Clause of Result	Qualifying verb *made* in A.
			COMPLEX SENTENCE	
5. A	he asked the women		Main Clause	Independent.
a¹	he had shut the gate behind him	when	Subord. Adv. Clause of Time	Qualifying verb *asked* in A.
a²	what they were doing there		Subord. Noun Clause	Object of verb *asked* in A.
			COMPLEX SENTENCE	

No.	Clause	Link	Kind	Function
6. A	the truth was		Main Clause	Independent.
a¹	they were seizing hats from the ware-house	that	Subord. Noun Clause	Complement to verb *was* in A.
a²	which apparently had no owner		Subord. Adj. Clause	Qualifying noun *warehouse* in a¹.
		COMPLEX SENTENCE		
7. A	they thought		Main Clause	Independent.
a¹	they might take possession of them	that	Subord. Noun Clause	Object to verb *thought* in A.
a²	no one else was there to claim them	as	Subord. Adv. Clause of Reason	Qualifying verb *take* in a¹.
		COMPLEX SENTENCE		
8. A	they were unconcerned and quiet		Main Clause	Independent.
a¹	they had been at a hatter's shop buying for their money	as if	Subord. Adv. Clause of Manner	Qualifying verb *were uncon-cerned* in A.
		COMPLEX SENTENCE		

Ex. 186.

No.	Clause	Link	Kind	Function
1. A	Mother chose the dress		Main Clause	Co-ordinate with B.
B	Father paid the bill	but	Main Clause	Co-ordinate with A.
		DOUBLE SENTENCE		
2. A	I asked no questions		Main Clause	Co-ordinate with B.
B	her chatter soon gave the game away	but	Main Clause	Co-ordinate with A.
		DOUBLE SENTENCE		

No.	Clause	Link	Kind	Function
3. A	you must work harder	either	Main Clause	Co-ordinate with B.
B	you will fail your examination	or	Main Clause	Co-ordinate with A.
		DOUBLE	SENTENCE	
4. A	the recruit was first interviewed by the sergeant		Main Clause	Co-ordinate with B.
B	who passed him on to a lieutenant		Main Clause	Co-ordinate with A.
		DOUBLE	SENTENCE	
5. A	we rowed	and	Main Clause	Co-ordinate with B and C.
B	(we) fished all the day		Main Clause	Co-ordinate with A and C.
C	no luck came our way	but	Main Clause	Co-ordinate with A and B.
		MULTIPLE	SENTENCE	
6. A	I may know (the young man)	and	Main Clause	Co-ordinate with B and C.
B	(I) may trust the young man		Main Clause	Co-ordinate with A and C.
C	he would not be my choice for you	but	Main Clause	Co-ordinate with A and B.
		MULTIPLE	SENTENCE	
7. A	Father entertained the children		Main Clause	Co-ordinate with B.
a¹	who makes an excellent Santa Claus		Subord. Adj. Clause	Qualifying noun *father* in A.
B	(Father) distributed the gifts	and	Main Clause	Co-ordinate with A.
		DOUBLE	SENTENCE	
8. A	the team returned to the home town	after	Main Clause	Co-ordinate with B.
a¹	the game was over		Subord. Adv. Clause of Time	Qualifying verb *returned* in A.
B	(the team) received a civic welcome	and	Main Clause	Co-ordinate with A.
b¹	they had brought the cup to the town for the first time	because	Subord. Adv. Clause of Reason	Qualifying verb *received* in B.
		DOUBLE	SENTENCE	

Ex. 187.

No.	Clause	Link	Kind	Function
1. A	men may come		Main Clause	Co-ordinate with B and C.
B	men may go	and	Main Clause	Co-ordinate with A and C.
C	I go on for ever	but	Main Clause	Co-ordinate with A and B.
			MULTIPLE SENTENCE	
2. A	the Mayor was dumb		Main Clause	Co-ordinate with B.
B	the Council stood	and	Main Clause	Co-ordinate with A.
b¹	they were changed into blocks of wood	as if	Subord. Adv. Clause of Manner	Qualifying verb *stood* in B.
			DOUBLE SENTENCE	
3. A	a man once declared		Main Clause	Co-ordinate with B.
a¹	he could lift himself into the air	that	Subord. Noun Clause	Object to verb *declared* in A.
B	his friends ridiculed the idea	but	Main Clause	Co-ordinate with A.
			DOUBLE SENTENCE	
4. A	green and blue his sharp eyes twinkled like a candle flame		Main Clause	Independent.
a¹	when salt is sprinkled		Subord. Adj. Clause	Qualifying noun *flame* in A.
			COMPLEX SENTENCE	
5. A	the hunters discovered		Main Clause	Independent,
a¹	the fox had made for Hinchlea woods	that	Subord. Noun Clause	Object to verb *discovered* (A).
a²	whom they had now been pursuing for four hours		Subord. Adj. Clause	Qualifying noun *fox* in a¹.
a³	where probably it could run to earth		Subord. Adj. Clause	Qualifying noun *woods* in a¹.
			COMPLEX SENTENCE	

No.	Clause	Link	Kind	Function
6. A	my assumption will be		Main Clause	Independent. [in A.
a¹	I hear from you by return of post	unless	Adv. Clause of Condition	Qualifying the verb *will be*
a²	you have refused the offer	that	Subord. Noun Clause	In apposition to noun *assumption*
a³	it is not generous enough	because	Subord. Adv. Clause of Reason	Qualifying verb *refused* in a².
		COMPLEX SENTENCE		
7. A	her finger was so small		Main Clause	Independent.
a¹	the ring would not stay on		Subord. Adv. Clause of Result	Qualifying *was so small* in A.
a²	which they did bring		Subord. Adj. Clause	Qualifying noun *ring* in a¹.
		COMPLEX SENTENCE		
8. A	I don't go much on religion		Main Clause	Co-ordinate with B and C.
B	I never ain't had no show		Main Clause	Co-ordinate with A and C.
C	I've got a middlin' tight grip on the handful o' things	but	Main Clause	Co-ordinate with A and B.
c¹	I know		Subord. Adj. Clause	Qualifying noun *things* in C.
		MULTIPLE SENTENCE		
9. A	I spake in a whisper as he		Main Clause	Co-ordinate with B.
a¹	who speaks in a room		Subord. Adj. Clause	Qualifying pronoun *he* in A.
a²	where someone is lying dead		Subord. Adj. Clause	Qualifying noun *room* in a¹.
B	he made no answer to	but	Main Clause	Co-ordinate with A.
b¹	what I said		Subord. Noun Clause	Object to preposition *to* in B.
		DOUBLE SENTENCE		
10. A	see		Main Clause	Co-ordinate with B and C.
a¹	thou keep		Subord. Noun Clause	Object of *see* in A.
a²	what he gives thee		Subord. Noun Clause	Object of *keep* in A.
B	stay not thou for food or sleep		Main Clause	Co-ordinate with A and C.
C	into it thou must not look	or	Main Clause	Co-ordinate with A and B.
c¹	be it scroll	{ Co-ord. Subord. Clauses of Condition		Qualifying verb *look* in C.
c²	be it book			
	Person addressed Knight	MULTIPLE SENTENCE		

No.	Clause	Link	Kind	Function
11. A	at Charing Cross, hard by the way, there is a house with stairs		Main Clause	Co-ordinate with B.
a¹	where we do sell our hay		Subord. Adj. Clause	Qualifying noun *house* in A.
B	there did I see coming down such folk, forty at least in pairs	and	Main Clause	Co-ordinate with A.
b²	as are not in our town		Subord. Adj. Clause	Qualifying noun *folk* in B.
	(thou know'st—Clause in parenthesis)		DOUBLE SENTENCE	
12. A	we did		Main Clause	Co-ordinate with B and C.
a¹	much as we chose to do		Subord. Adv. Clause of Manner	Qualifying verb *did* in A.
B	we'd never heard of Mrs. Grundy		Main Clause	Co-ordinate with A and C.
C	all the theology was	that	Main Clause	Co-ordinate with A and B.
b¹	we knew		Subord. Adj. Clause	Qualifying noun *theology* (C).
b²	we mightn't play on Sunday	that	Subord. Noun Clause	Complement to verb *was* (C).
			DOUBLE SENTENCE	
13. A	that day a blizzard overtook them with such violence		Main Clause	
a¹	Scott, realising, pitched camp	that	Subord. Adv. Clause of Result co-ordinate with a²	Qualifying verb *overtook* in A.
a²	(Scott) stayed there	and	Subord. Adv. Clause of Result co-ordinate with a¹	Qualifying verb *overtook* in A.
a³	they had marched for half an hour	when	Subord. Adv. Clause of Time	Qualifying verb *pitched* in a¹.
a⁴	no one of them could face such weather	that	Subord. Noun Clause	Object to verb *realising* in a¹.
a⁵	the weather improved	until	Subord. Adv. Clause of Time	Qualifying verb *stayed* in a².
			COMPLEX SENTENCE	

No.	Clause	Link	Kind	Function
14. A	Master John will become		Main Clause	Co-ordinate with B.
a¹	he very quickly mends his ways	unless	Subord. Adv. Clause of Condition	Qualifying verb *will become* in A.
a²	what his father was before him		Subord. Noun Subject Clause	Complement to verb *will become* in A.
B	the Court will treat him as severely	and	Main Clause	Co-ordinate with A.
b¹	it did his father	as	Subord. Adv. Clause of Manner	Qualifying verb *treat* in B.
		DOUBLE	SENTENCE	
15. A	snug in my easy chair, I stirred the fire to flame		Main Clause	Co-ordinate with B and C.
B	I shut my eyes to heat and light	and	Main Clause	Co-ordinate with A and C.
C	(I) saw in sudden night crouched in the dripping dark, with steaming shoulders stark, the man		Main Clause	Co-ordinate with A and B.
c¹	who hews the coal to feed my fire		Subord. Adj. Clause	Qualifying noun **man** in C.
		MULTIPLE	SENTENCE	
16. A	her tongue was not less keen than her eye		Main Clause	Co-ordinate with B.
B	(her tongue) seemed to take up an unfinished lecture precisely at the point	and	Main Clause	Co-ordinate with A.
b¹	a damsel came within earshot	whenever	Subord. Adv. Clause of Time	Qualifying verb *seemed to take* in B.
b²	a barrel-organ takes up a tune	as	Subord. Adv. Clause of Manner	Qualifying verb *seemed to take* in B.
b³	where it had left off		Subord. Adj. Clause	Qualifying noun *point* in B.
		DOUBLE	SENTENCE	

No.	Clause	Link	Kind	Function
17. A	the albatross was undisturbed for some time		Main Clause	Co-ordinate with B and C.
a^1	the noise of our bows, gradually approaching, roused him	until	Subord. Adv. Clause of Time	Qualifying verb *was undisturbed* in A.
B	lifting his head he stared upon us for a moment	when	Main Clause	Co-ordinate with A, C and D.
C	then (he) spread his wide wings	and	Main Clause	Co-ordinate with A, B and D.
D	(he) took his flight	and	Main Clause	Co-ordinate with A, B and C.
			MULTIPLE SENTENCE	
18. A	the rumour had become so widespread	that	Main Clause	In app. to noun *rumour* in A.
a^1	the Prime Minister was to resign	that	Subord. Noun Clause	Qualifying verb *had become* in A.
a^2	it was being discussed in every village in England		Subord. Adv. Clause of Result	
			COMPLEX SENTENCE	
19. A	the dealer then approached the farmer, finding		Main Clause	Independent.
a^1	his first quest was in vain	**that**	Subord. Noun Clause	Object of participle *finding* in A.
a^2	who would sell some of his pedigree herd		Subord. Adj. Clause	Qualifying noun *farmer* in A.
a^3	he hoped		Clause in parenthesis	
a^4	which was the pride of the district		Subord. Adj. Clause	Qualifying noun *herd* in a^2.
			COMPLEX SENTENCE	
20. A	he throws down the reins with something of an air		Main Clause	Co-ordinate with B.
a^1	he arrives	when	Subord. Adj. Clause of Time	Qualifying verb *throws* in A.
a^2	the horses are to be changed	where	Subord. Adv. Clause of Place	Qualifying verb *arrives* in a^1.
B	(he) abandons the cattle to **the care** of an hostler	and	Main Clause	Co-ordinate with A.
b^1	his duty is merely to drive from one stage to another	as	Subord. Adv. Clause of Reason	Qualifying verb *abandons* in B.
			DOUBLE SENTENCE	

Revision

No.	Clause	Link	Kind	Function
1. A¹	No one can predict		Main Clause co-ord. with A²	Object of verb *can predict* (A¹) and *can imagine* (A²).
A²	no one can even imagine		Main Clause co-ord. with A¹	
a¹	how this terrible war against German and Nazi aggression will run its course		Subord. Noun Clause co-ord. with a² and a³	Object of verb *can predict* (A¹) and *can imagine* (A²).
a²	how far it will spread	or	Subord. Noun Clause co-ord. with a² and a³	Object of verb *can predict* (A¹) and *can imagine* (A²).
a³	how long it will last	or	Subord. Noun Clause co-ord. with a² and a³	
		DOUBLE	SENTENCE	
B	Long, dark months of trials and tribulations lie before us		SIMPLE SENTENCE.	Independent.
C	Not only great dangers but many more misfortunes, many short-comings, many mistakes, many disappointments will surely be our lot		SIMPLE SENTENCE	Independent.
D	Death and sorrow will be the companions of our journey, hardship our garment, constancy and valour our only shield		SIMPLE SENTENCE	Independent.

No.	Clause	Link	Kind	Function
E^1	We must be united		Main Clause co-ord. with E^2 and E^1	
E^2	we must be undaunted		Main Clause co-ord. with E^1 and E^3	
E^3	we must be inflexible	MULTIPLE SENTENCE	Main Clause co-ord. with E^2 and E^3	
F^1	Our qualities and deeds must burn		Main Clause co-ord. with F^2	
F^2	(they must) glow through the gloom of Europe	and	Main Clause co-ord. with F^1	
f^2	they become the inevitable beacon of its salvation	until, DOUBLE SENTENCE	Subord. Adv. Clause of Time	Qualifying verb *must break* (F^1) and *must glow* (F^2).

2. *aggression.* Noun, Abstract, Singular, Accusative Case, governed by preposition " against."

far. Adverb of Place, qualifying verb " will spread."

will last. Verb, Active, Intransitive, Weak, 3rd Person Singular, Future Simple, forming predicate to pronoun " it."

more. Adjective of Quantity, Comparative degree, qualifying noun " misfortunes."

our. Adjective, Possessive, qualifying noun " garment."

through. Preposition, governing noun " gloom," forming phrase " through the gloom."

until. Conjunction joining Clauses " Our qualities . . . Europe " with " then become . . . salvation."

beacon. Noun, Common, Singular, Nominative Case, complement to verb " become."

Ex. 189.

1. Full stop at *Italian, Englishman.*

2. Full stop at *firm, door, Navee.*

Ex. 191.

1. Commas at *Roche, statements, said, alone.* Full stop at *greater.*

2. Commas at *recently, ceremony, bridegroom, remarked, everyone, unfortunately.* Full stop at *thing, recently, said.*

Ex. 192.

but, whole, himself, stature, him ; use tools, devise tools ; before him ; iron, paste ; highway, without tools ; without tools, he is nothing ; with tools, he is all.

Ex. 194.

1. temporary. It . . . moment ; but . . . subduing again : governed, conquered.

2. 'Tis the voice of the lobster ; I heard him declare, " You have baked me too brown, I must sugar my hair."

3. 1 . . . American . . . London, . . . delicious, nourish-

ing, food, stewed, roasted, baked, boiled, fricassee, ragout.

4. What was to be done ?—'Twas perfectly plain
That they could not well hang the man over again !
What was to be done ?—The man was dead !
Nought could be done—nought could be said ;
So—my Lord Tomnoddy went home to bed.

5. "Do you spell it with a 'v' or a 'w'?" inquired the judge. "That depends upon the taste and fancy of the speller, my lord," replied Sam.

6. At Godwin's they (Lamb, Holcroft and Coleridge) were disputing fiercely which was the better—Man as he was, or man as he is to be. "Give me," says Lamb, "man as he is not to be." This saying . . . us, . . . continues.

Ex. 195.

"Ride . . . there's a letter for me," said . . . Andy.
"Yes, sir."
"You . . . go ? "
"To . . . town, sir."
"But . . . town ? "
"No, sir."
"And why don't you ask, . . . thief ? "
"Sure, I'd find out, sir."
"Did not . . . you're . . . don't know ? "
"Yes, sir."
"And why don't you ? "
"I don't . . . troublesome, sir."
"Confound you," said the squire ; though . . . Andy's . . . ignorance.
"Well," continued he, "go to the post office. You . . . office, I suppose ? "
"Yes, sir, . . . gunpowder."
"You're right for once," said the squire ; for His Majesty's Postmaster was the person . . . combustible. "Go, then, to the post office, . . . me. Remember—not gunpowder, but a letter."
"Yes, sir," said Andy, who got . . . hack, . . . post office. On arriving . . . postmaster (for that . . . groceries,

gimlets, broadcloth, and linen drapery), Andy . . . counter, and said :

" I want a letter, sir, if you please."

" Who . . . for ? " said the postmaster, in a tone . . . life : so . . . question.

" I want a letter, sir, if you please."

" And who do you want it for ? " repeated the postmaster.

" What's that to you ? " said Andy.

The postmaster, laughing . . . simplicity, told . . . directions.

" The directions I got . . . letter here—that's the directions."

" Who gave you those directions ? "

" The master."

" And who's your master ? "

" What concern is that o' yours ? "

Revision

1. For abbreviations.

2. By commas, by brackets, by dashes.

3. (i) By a colon. (ii) In some older forms of writing by a comma, followed by a capital. (iii) By :—

4. Cf. Section " Capital Letters," Chapter XIV.

5. Give me what I have, or even less ; and therewith let me live to myself for what remains of life, if the gods will that anything remain. Let me have a generous supply of books and of food stored for a year ahead ; nor let me hang and tremble on the hope of the uncertain hour. Nay, it is enough to ask Jove, who gives them and takes them away, that he grant life and subsistence ; a balanced mind I will find for myself.